Routledge Revivals

Religious Thought in France in the Nineteenth Century

First published in 1935, *Religious Thought in France in the Nineteenth Century* discusses various religious thoughts prevalent in France during the nineteenth century, along with prominent figures associated with them. The author explores Positivist Religion, Natural Religion, and Older and Newer Protestantism. He then talks about the modernist movement in France through the life and career of distinguished critic Alfred Loisy. The author goes on to examine the future of religion and the influence of Bergson and provides a commentary on the biblical and historical studies among Catholics, Catholic studies of Dogma, and the preachers in Paris like Mgr. de Quélen, Jesuit Ravignan, Jesuit Félix, Père Hyacinthe and Monsabré, to name a few. Simpson concludes his book with a discussion on the influence of Church on literary men – Bourget, Huysmans, Faguet, and Brunetière.

Religious Thought in France in the Nineteenth Century

Canon W. J. Sparrow Simpson

First published in 1935
by George Allen & Unwin Ltd

This edition first published in 2024 by Routledge
4 Park Square, Milton Park, Abingdon, Oxon, OX14 4RN

and by Routledge
605 Third Avenue, New York, NY 10017

Routledge is an imprint of the Taylor & Francis Group, an informa business

© 1935 Canon W. J. Sparrow Simpson

All rights reserved. No part of this book may be reprinted or reproduced or utilised in any form or by any electronic, mechanical, or other means, now known or hereafter invented, including photocopying and recording, or in any information storage or retrieval system, without permission in writing from the publishers.

Publisher's Note
The publisher has gone to great lengths to ensure the quality of this reprint but points out that some imperfections in the original copies may be apparent.

Disclaimer
The publisher has made every effort to trace copyright holders and welcomes correspondence from those they have been unable to contact.

A Library of Congress record exists under LCCN: 35008958

ISBN: 978-1-032-85205-8 (hbk)
ISBN: 978-1-003-51709-2 (ebk)
ISBN: 978-1-032-85207-2 (pbk)

Book DOI 10.4324/9781003517092

Canon W. J. Sparrow Simpson

Religious Thought in France
in the
Nineteenth Century

LONDON
GEORGE ALLEN & UNWIN LTD
MUSEUM STREET

FIRST PUBLISHED IN 1935

All rights reserved
PRINTED IN GREAT BRITAIN BY
UNWIN BROTHERS LTD., WOKING

CONTENTS

CHAPTER		PAGE
I.	The Positivist Religion	9
II.	Natural Religion in France	24
III.	The Older Protestantism in France	29
IV.	The Newer Protestantism in France	39
V.	The Newer Protestantism on the Deity of Christ	47
VI.	The Newer Protestantism on Redemption	69
VII.	The Newer Protestantism on the Nature of the Church	78
VIII.	The Issues of Modernism in France	89
IX.	The Future of Religion	107
X.	The Influence of Bergson	122
XI.	Biblical and Historical Studies among Catholics in France	129
XII.	Catholic Studies of Dogma in France	139
XIII.	Preachers in Paris in the Nineteenth Century	155
XIV.	The Literary Men attracted to the Church	178
	Index	187

Religious Thought in France in the Nineteenth Century

CHAPTER I

The Positivist Religion

THE early years of Auguste Comte, founder of the Positivist Religion, were spent in the beginning of the nineteenth century. The atmosphere of his home was Catholic. But he informs us that from the age of thirteen he had broken with the religious beliefs of his people. He divided his maturity into two distinct careers. According to Levy-Bruhl,* one of his ablest exponents, Comte asserted "without affected modesty" that in his first career he was Aristotle, and in his second he will be S. Paul. "I have systematically devoted my life," he said, "to draw at last from real science the necessary basis of a sound philosophy, according to which I was afterwards to construct the true Religion." Levy-Bruhl confines attention to Comte's first career. "Many of Comte's disciples, even some of the more illustrious, and at first more fervent, such as Littré, refused to follow him in his second career. Their

* Levy-Bruhl, *The Philosophy of Comte*, p. 5.

admiration for the philosopher could not induce them to submit to the pontiff."

The positive philosophy harmonized to a considerable degree with the scientific spirit of the age. Comte's fellow-countryman, Levy-Bruhl, calls attention to the remarkable fact that "of all the systems which found birth in France in the nineteenth century, this one alone found a hearing beyond the frontiers, and left a deep impression upon foreign thinkers." Comte's philosophy was at first received in England even with more sympathy than in France. "John Stuart Mill, Herbert Spencer, George Lewes, George Eliot, and a number of English philosophers and writers drew more or less of their inspiration from it."

Comte was of course convinced that the positive philosophy was verified and proved. He laid great stress on intellectual demonstration. It is significant that at the same time he recognized the value of faith. He declared that the great majority of men will always have to take on faith the conclusions of positive philosophy. Men privileged with sufficient leisure, and endowed with sufficient culture, to examine these conclusions and to investigate their proofs, will, he thought, always be few. The attitude of others must be one of submission and respect. Comte pointed out that his philosophy was in a similar position to that of scientific theories which the generality of men accept but cannot prove. Comparatively few men are competent to understand the arguments on which the

The Positivist Religion

Copernican theory of the solar system depends. They know, however, that what is for them only a matter of faith is for certain other persons a matter of science. They know that what is for them a matter of faith would become a matter of science, if they had gone through the necessary studies enabling them to reach that certainty. It is obvious, therefore, that knowledge is only for the intellectual few, while faith is the inevitable condition for the vast majority. Comte's assertion is that if all minds were in a condition to examine the dogmas of that faith, all, without exception, would understand the demonstration, and would agree with it.

According to Comte, the fundamental law of human progress is that the race advances through three successive states: the theological, the metaphysical, and the scientific. To this last he gave the name of Positivism. It was concerned with all the phenomena of existence accessible to human investigation. The theological state was that condition in which the realm of phenomena was explained by the action and will of Deities. It was the state in which natural phenomena were attributed to supernatural causes. Thus for Comte the theological state was the period of the fictitious and imaginary, the mythological and unreal. The metaphysical state was, in Comte's valuation, not much superior. It differed from the former by attributing phenomena to invariable laws, instead of supernatural personalities. It is abstract and theoretical, and less effective than the former. The positive or scientific state was confined within the realm of the natural, and occupied the entire sphere of that which is in reality ascertainable by man. The first or theological state was the necessary starting-place for human intelligence. The third is its fixed and final state. The second is only a state of transition from the elementary to the complete and perfect form of human knowledge.

II

Guizot's account of Comte is well known, but too important to be omitted. Comte in Guizot's opinion was "single-minded, honest, of profound convictions, devoted to his own ideas, in appearance modest, although at heart prodigiously vain; he sincerely believed that it was his calling to open a new era for the mind of man and for human society. Whilst listening to him, I could hardly refrain from expressing my astonishment that a mind so vigorous should at the same time be so narrow, as not even to perceive the nature and bearing of the facts with which he was dealing, and the questions which he was authoritatively deciding; that a character so disinterested should not be warned by his own proper sentiments —which were moral in spite of his system—of its falsity and its negation of morality. I did not even make any attempt at discussion with M. Comte: his sincerity, his enthusiasm, and the delusion that blinded

The Positivist Religion

him, inspired me with that sad esteem that takes refuge in silence."*

In his later years Comte became convinced of the necessity of some emotional expression of his principles. Accordingly he created in the years 1851-1854 a new Religion.

The essential principles of Religion consisted, according to Comte, of two Dogmas: God and Immortality. Comte attempted to place on both Dogmas a Positivist interpretation. Thus God represented the idea of a Universal Being, eternal, with which human souls communicate, and which infuses power to unite them. Immortality is the ascription to good men of a share in the eternal life of the Divine Being.

Positivism rejected both the personality of God and the personal immortality of men. But Comte was satisfied that Positivism could provide an equivalent for the two fundamental Dogmas of Religion. That equivalent was Humanity. It is not an abstraction. It consists of all that men have thought and felt and accomplished in the direction of the good and noble and eternal. Therefore Humanity is the real Deity that men require. It is the Great Being which raises us above ourselves. The idea of Humanity Comte found most inspiring, appealing to our sympathetic instincts, and overcoming our egotistic tendencies. Moreover, Humanity is the real equivalent to Immortality. For it consists of the thoughts and virtues of actual men,

* Guizot, *Memoires*, iii, pp. 125-127.

and it consists far more largely of the dead than of the living.

Comte of course acknowledged that this Deity was not personal, and this Immortality was not the perpetuation of individual existence; but he refused to admit that Religion properly understood was at all destroyed by this difference.

Accordingly, he constructed what he called the Religion of Humanity. He published a whole series of volumes on social and religious matters, together with a Calendar of Saints, and a Catechism of the Positivist Religion. His fellow-countryman, Caro, says that Comte did not discuss: he pontificated. He no longer wrote letters, but issued Briefs. He inaugurated Sacraments—marriage and so forth. And what Huxley called "Catholicism minus Christianity" was launched upon the world. Several of Comte's eminent disciples were unable to follow the Master in these developments. The subordination of the mind to the heart, the theocratic policy, the return to a new theological period, was too much for them.

Of this Positivist Religion, the Religion of Humanity, Emile Boutroux* was one of the severest critics. Comte was subject to mental and emotional aberrations. His infatuation for Clotilde de Vaux was published in language which has disconcerted many of his admirers. But quite apart from complications of that nature, the Religion of Humanity was itself nothing more than

* Boutroux, *Science et Religion*, p. 53.

The Positivist Religion

fiction and imagination. For since, according to the Positivist Philosophy, there was no such thing as personal Immortality, the Positivist Religion created for the dead nothing more than a survival in the memory and imagination of the living. According to the Positivist Philosophy mankind had escaped from the stage of theology into that of science. According to the Positivist Religion it returned to the religious and theological conceptions from which it had escaped.

One of Comte's most distinguished disciples was Emile Littré, compiler of the great French Dictionary. He was for a while a Deist of the eighteenth-century type, believing in God, the soul, and immortality. But his Deism disappeared. Apparently it had never been more than a philosophic idea. His real interest was restricted to that which was scientifically verifiable. He came to regard theologies as a natural product of human evolution. He was not altogether without experience of religious emotions. He declares that he neither refused them nor disdained them. But they were not spontaneous in his soul. In conversation with believers he drew a contrast between *my* evidence which causes me to reject this theological Dogma, and *your* evidence which causes you to accept it. Thus religion was reduced to psychology.

An admirable critical account of Littré and his philosophical and religious ideas is that by Caro of the French Academy, published in 1883. Caro relates

Religious Thought in France

how Littré, at the mature age of forty, encountered the Positivist Philosophy of Auguste Comte. Positivism had existed already some fourteen years. Its analysis of human progress into three successive stages: theological, philosophical, scientific, had much to commend itself to a century conscious of its advance in science. And Littré was simply fascinated by the six volumes of the Positivist Philosophy. That was in 1840. He became one of Comte's most able and ardent advocates and exponents, and adhered all through his life to the Positivist outlook.

Caro considers that at the time he himself was writing, that is in 1883, Positivism, in the form which Comte expounded and Littré received, was practically dead, but yet in the political world it was more alive than ever, and was in a fair way to become the official philosophy of France.

A frequently quoted incident in Littré's married life throws light upon his character. His wife was a religious-minded woman, and in spite of her husband's scepticism had brought up their daughter in the Christian Religion. The daughter was intellectually gifted, and became a valuable aid to her father in his studies. Littré had respected his wife's religion, and consented to leave the education of the daughter in her control. He had intended, when the girl arrived at a sufficiently developed stage of intellectual inquiry, to explain to her his own convictions. However, when the time arrived, he realized that his daughter was

The Positivist Religion

undoubtedly adapted to Religion. Her convictions were very real, and he had not the heart to make any effort to disturb what was so evidently the actual foundation of her life. As he had respected his wife's religion, so also he respected his daughter's. After all, his attitude towards the Supernatural was that of the Agnostic. The Agnostic holds his judgment in suspense with regard to the momentous problem of the existence of a Divine Intelligence. It was a question which he neither affirmed nor denied. Theoretically, therefore, he adopted an attitude of impartial indecision between the Scylla and Charybdis of yes and no. How then could he consistently impose a negative upon his daughter in a matter where he was constrained on principle to own that he did not really know?

Next to Littré may be placed Hippolyte Taine. He was not a disciple of Positivism, but he is eminently characteristic of French free thought in the generation which followed that of Comte. Taine's countrymen seem greatly divided about his character. According to one critic no man was less religious than Hippolyte Taine.* According to another he was one of those happy souls who seem naturally attracted to what is morally right.† According to a third critic‡—not a fellow-countryman—he is a scientific positivist, a disillusioned romanticist, and his whole work is pervaded by the bitter flavour of this disillusion.

* Faguet. † Stapfer.
‡ Irving Babbitt, p. 233.

Religious Thought in France

Taine had no belief in the freedom of the will, but considered that its absence did not exclude moral responsibility. Among his trusted guides were Spinoza and Marcus Aurelius. A study of Hegel daily for a year resulted in a fervid declaration in which he pictured the German philosopher as Spinoza multiplied by Aristotle, and seated on that pyramid of sciences which modern experience during the last three centuries has erected. This verdict was somewhat sobered by maturer reconsideration, but Hegel's conception of the Universe was still represented as the greatest and the highest, and declared to have conferred effective incentives to virtue to a multitude of souls.

It is singular that Taine should be author of the remark that vice and virtue are products like vitriol and sugar. It does not, however, appear that he intended that proposition, which Victor Hugo indignantly resented, to be interpreted in the sense in which it has been naturally taken. Nothing was more repugnant to Taine than moral indifference. He appealed to the conscience of the naturalist school of romance against the disastrous effect of sensual deceptions.*

It is said that his experience of religion in England modified the severity of his atheistic dogmatism. Later in life—it was in 1892—he reflected that it is possible that scientific truth is unwholesome for the human

* Paul Stapfer, *L'Inquiétude Religieuse*, pp. 151-187.

The Positivist Religion

animal, from which he drew the conclusion that it is only for certain persons that scientific truth is bearable. Some were able to reconcile the scientific spirit with the religious, but in France those who left Catholicism were able to find no intermediary stopping-places between Catholicism and Free Thought. There was much in the practical devotions of Catholics in France which revolted Taine. Yet there were times when he could become lyrical in praise of the achievements of the Christian Religion, as the following famous passage proves:*

"At this very day, after eighteen centuries . . . Christianity works as heretofore in the artisans of Galilee and in the selfsame way, to replace the love of others for the love of self. Neither its essence nor its methods are changed. Whether its form is Greek or Catholic or Protestant, it is still for four hundred millions of human beings, the spiritual organ, the great pair of wings indispensable to raise a man above himself. . . . Always and everywhere, in these eighteen centuries, as soon as these wings fail private and public morals suffer deterioration . . . When this spectacle is before us, we can estimate the value of Christianity in modern society, the modesty, the sweetness, the humaneness it has introduced, the support it gives to good faith, to right. Neither philosophic reason, nor artistic and literary culture, nor even a sense of honour, whether feudal, military, or chivalrous, no

* *Origines du régime moderne*, T. III, pp. 146-147.

code, no administration, no form of government can suffice to supply its place in this service. There is nothing but it to detain us on the fatal slope, and to arrest the unconscious decline by which perpetually, and with all the weight of our origin, our race sinks backward towards its lowest beginnings. The ancient Gospel, under whatever form it is offered, is still to this day the finest supporter of the social instincts of man."

Taine's splendid tribute to the value of the Christian Religion down the centuries did not hinder him from criticism of great severity on the actual condition of Catholicism in France, and its more recent development. He held that the two principal Dogmas decreed about that time were exactly constructed to obstruct for ever a reconciliation between science and faith. At the same time he drew distinctions. As to Religion, he wrote, "what seems to me inconsistent with modern science is not Christianity but Roman Catholicism as it now exists." With Liberal Protestantism on the contrary reconciliation was possible.

When Taine became the father of a family he saw that his children were instructed in Religion. To a Freethinker who criticized his action he replied—"You will understand when you have a family of your own." Stapfer says that it was to Protestantism that he turned for his children's teachers, not to Catholicism. But Victor Giraud records that Taine himself is said in educating his children to have given them one of

The Positivist Religion

Pascal's Provincial Letters, or a Sermon of Bourdalone to analyse.*

The Positivist Philosophy possessed for a time distinguished adherents in England; but the Positivist Religion divided them into two sharply opposing camps. Such men as John Stuart Mill and Frederic Harrison repudiated all association with this substitute for Religion, while Congreve encouraged and supported it. Some few selected souls, contemplating their own personal extinction at death at least as probable, aspired to join the Choir Invisible which would survive in the memory of the subsequent generations. But the Positivist Religion, according to its own adherents, was never a success. A strange account of its condition in England can be read in the *Memoir of a Positivist* by Malcolm Quin.

It seems that a Church of Humanity was set up in Newcastle, where, however, the Unbelievers professed an inability to conceive how a Religion without a God could find a place for prayer. The Church of Humanity contained an Altar, above which hung a reproduction of the Sistine Madonna. Before it were seven lights symbolizing the seven master sciences of Humanity. There was added a Crucifix and a Statue of the Virgin Mother, and a tablet of the Ten Commandments in Hebrew. An Apostle of the Positivist Religion officiated as priest. But the "emancipated congregation," which was small and "chiefly com-

* V. Giraud, p. 31.

posed of Freethinkers, drawn largely from Protestant sects," found kneeling a trial, and "there was something for everybody to dislike." However, there was a comfortable feeling of being delivered from "the metaphysical jargon of a lapsed mythology." The audience appreciated the Symbol of the Mother and Child, "even as Raphael paints it." But when the Positivist Apostle had done his best to explain the Religion of Humanity, the people "somehow seemed to care no more about it." They liked the idea of a Religion without Theology, but nobody seemed to want it in the form of Positivism. "Perhaps," says the writer, "they thought the remedy was worse than the disease." Comte's own definition of prayer is "Commemoration followed by effusion": to which a sceptical critic retorted, "effuse as much as you like, but why call it prayer." This Positivizing of Catholicism was carried further still. A festival of the Virgin Mother was held on the same day as the Festival of the Assumption, and its observance led to a celebration of the Festival of the Nativity on Christmas Day. This innovation led to open protest and secession. But what produced a more serious crisis in the little group was a travesty of the Mass. The minister pontificated before the group of Freethinkers from the Protestant sects, with the result that the congregation melted away and the experiment was admitted to be a dismal failure. The Church of Humanity was closed, and replaced by a Synagogue of the Jews. This was

The Positivist Religion

in the year 1910. The Vestments went to the Priory of S. Dominic, and the historic busts adorned a local Grammar School. Such was the singular experience in England of the Positivist Religion. The disappointed Apostle of the Positivist Religion then visited Paris, made a pilgrimage to the grave of Comte, and visited the Positivist Church which, he observed, was waiting for a congregation.

CHAPTER II

Natural Religion in France

DURING the first half of the nineteenth century there arose in France what Guizot described as a Spiritualist School of Philosophy. It disregarded supernatural Revelation, and endeavoured to establish Theistic principles through the speculative exercise of Reason. This School of writers greatly contributed to promote belief in the three great doctrines of the freedom of the human will, the existence of God, and the prospect of Immortality. Thus it supplied to a certain extent the craving for Religion. It was, however, generally intellectualist rather than religious, concerned with conclusions of the reason rather than with the practices of devotion.

Among the best representatives of this Spiritualist Philosophy were Victor Cousin, Emile Saisset, Jules Simon, Caro and Paul Janet.

Guizot, their contemporary, considered that these writers had rendered valuable service to the cause of Religion. The moral freedom of man involved his responsibility for the formation of his own character and the determination of his own destiny. But this School of Theism philosophized irrespectively of all positive revelation. Their Natural Religion, their religious philosophy was no substitute for Christianity.

Natural Religion in France

Victor Cousin was an eclectic thinker. He has been represented as an advocate of academic rationalism. His *Histoire de la Philosophie* was condemned to the Index in 1844 by Gregory XVI. Reissued under a revised form and an altered title—*Du Vrai, du Beau, du Bien*—it was again condemned. Bellamy says that at the request of some of the French Episcopate, especially Mgr. Sibour, Archbishop of Paris, out of consideration for Cousin, the second condemnation was not published.

Caro was well known for his book—*L'Idée de Dieu**—in which he subjected to a searching analysis the critical school represented by Renan, which reduced facts to ideals, and reason to sentiment; the revival of Naturalism represented by Taine; and the Duty of Idealism represented by Vacherot.

Jules Simon, in his admirable book *Le Devoir*,† had spent seventeen years in professional teaching, and published the result of his reflections in the conviction that belief in Duty requires belief in God, in freedom, and in Immortality. He insisted that it was opportune to remind men of their duties at a time when most of them were exclusively absorbed about their rights, and when their rights were often confused with their self-interest. Moral Truths were no arbitrary decisions of Omnipotence, but based upon the essential nature of God.

One of the most attractive exponents of Natural

---

* 1864.   † Fourth Edition, 1856.

Religious Thought in France

Religion in France about 1840 was Emile Saisset, professor of Philosophy in Paris.

In an interesting autobiographical account Saisset explained the process of his own development, his outlook on religious life in France, and the motives which prompted him to write on religious Philosophy. Brought up in a Christian atmosphere he became a student of Spinoza and felt the attractiveness of the Pantheistic interpretation of existence: Deity represented the immanent principles of evolution, nature the manifestation of that principle. The impersonal principle emerged in each of its productions. Thus God sleeps in the mineral, dreams in the animal, wakens in the man.

That interpretation is confronted and refuted by the fact of Personality. Influenced by his Christian education Saisset says that he had never seriously questioned the Personality of God. German philosophy imported into France was undermining that belief. Fichte declared Personality was a limitation, limitation could not be attributed to the Ultimate Being, the idea of God should therefore be left undetermined. Yet it was unquestionably true that man is so constituted that nothing finite can suffice him. He looks beyond the material universe in search of an ideal and perfect object of love, and hope, and adoration. Saisset was convinced that such a being could not acquiesce in the constructions of German Pantheism. Neither could such a being rest in the attitude of agnosticism which neither affirms nor denies and has nothing to say about the nature of the Ultimate Reality. To Saisset's mind the vital question for the nineteenth century was the question of the Divine Personality. To that question he devoted all his powers of reflection.

And the results of his Meditations are given in his *Essay on Religious Philosophy*. The book is a memorable endeavour to establish on spiritual grounds the inadequacy of any impersonal First Principle to account for the facts of human nature. The book was translated into English in 1863. Saisset was a Platonist well read in S. Augustine, whose work on the City of God he translated into French. Saisset's philosophic Essay is memorable for sustained elevation of thought and profoundly religious spirit.

Of the Scepticism prevalent in France, Saisset said: "My profound conviction is that this negative philosophy is a disease of our times, a bitter fruit of our philosophical disputes." The Divine existence is not capable of demonstration owing to the weakness of the human intellect.

Saisset maintained that the arguments for the existence of God contributed towards belief in His Reality. They were cumulative reasonings. There were Truths, said Saisset, which could be attained by Reason. And there were Truths that could only be attained by Intuition. The existence of the perfection of Personality was a Truth of the latter kind. It was like the Truth of Freewill. It is a direct intuition, but it is not the conclusion of a syllogism. This confidence in spiritual intuition is memorable.

The writings of Emile Saisset display a spiritual insight and a religious disposition which enabled him to guide his contemporaries in the direction of rudimentary Theism, and which, if he had been convinced of the Truth of Supernatural Revelation, would have made him an outstanding leader in Religion. As it was, he became a power, not only over his own countrymen. The influence of this School of Spiritualist Philosophy was felt in England, and can be seen in Anglican writers of that time.

CHAPTER III

The Older Protestantism in France

CATHOLICISM is unquestionably the Religion of France. When a Frenchman is religious he is almost invariably a Catholic. Napoleon is reported to have perpetrated the cynical remark that there was not enough Religion in France to make two. Yet there is a Protestant element in France. It is a mere minority, and apparently does not increase. According to its critics it has no corporate power.* It is essentially individualist with no united Creed. It is a Religion subjected to free examination from each of its independent adherents. There is no question of Protestantism in France. At the same time what must impress any inquirer into the religious thought of that great Nation is that Protestantism among French-speaking people has produced a remarkable succession of distinguished influential leaders, out of all proportion to its numerical insignificance.

All through the nineteenth century Protestant writers of France have been well known in other countries than their own, in England conspicuously. The works of such men as Vinet, Sabatier, Réville, and many others, have had considerable influence in English Religion. And the progress of Protestant thought in France provides significant instruction. The tendencies

* Guignebert, *Le Probléme Religieux*, p. xii.

of Protestantism in modern life may be advantageously studied in another nation than our own. The literature is abundant.

I

Alexandre Vinet is claimed by Guizot to belong to France as much as to Switzerland, and to have served the cause of religious liberty and the reaction to Christianity in France not less than in Switzerland. As to the divine origin of Christianity and its fundamental dogmas, Vinet, in Guizot's opinion, never had the least hesitation, and never made the smallest concession. This estimate may well be thought to need considerable qualification. Vinet's dominant interests were in the direction of personal religious sentiment rather than in that of definite dogma on which that sentiment is based.

II

Orthodox Protestantism may be found admirably illustrated in the writings of Grétillat, Professor of Theology in the independent Faculty at Neuchatel.

Grétillat's *Théologie Systématique*, published in four volumes between the years 1885 and 1890, is an exposition of Evangelical Doctrine. It is a characteristic and important example of the older Scholastic Protestantism, remarkable for its adherence in many essential matters to the ancient traditional faith of a Christian. It gives an orthodox exposition of the doctrine of

The Older Protestantism in France

the Holy Trinity. It is well acquainted with and highly critical of the German theological deviations from the historic faith, especially of the Tubingen School.

Following the older Evangelical traditions, Grétillat taught the identity of the Historic Christ and the Second Person of the Holy Trinity. The Self in Christ was the self of the Divine Son of God. His pre-existence was eternal. This was rested on the teaching of Christ and His Apostles. Thus the Protestant School at Neuchatel was instructed in the unaltered doctrine of the Divine Incarnation. Considerable use was made by Grétillat of Godet's well-known Commentary on S. John. The doctrine of the self-limitation of the Son of God, the Kenosis, found an able supporter in Grétillat. Redemption is expounded on historic lines. Much is said on the sacerdotal office of Christ and the doctrine of Propitiation. Grétillat maintained that Reparation for sin was necessary towards God; that the Cross was an objective satisfaction or reparation godward, and that this godward offering was necessitated by the moral character of Deity. The sin of man did not only inflict injury on human nature, but also on the obligation of man towards God. This Godward aspect of Redemption was involved in Romans v. 10. We were reconciled while we were objects of Divine aversion. The Father took the initiative in providing the priestly function of Christ. The Death of Christ is not only a reconciliation of the world with God, but also an expiation ($\iota\lambda\alpha\sigma\mu\delta s$)

for the sin of the whole world (1 S. John ii. 2). Grétillat was well aware of the inadequacy of all human repentance. Who is to judge whether my repentance is adequate to secure my forgiveness? Is it myself?

The priesthood of Christ is concentrated in the closing scenes of His earthly life. He is the supreme Mediator between God and humanity. The Crucifixion is an offering and a Sacrifice to God. "Never did incense more acceptable arise from earth to Heaven."

Grétillat rejects entirely the Calvinistic theory of the attitude of the Father towards His Crucified Son. He is also most emphatic that the Passion of Christ was no substitution of Christ for men, but a self-identity of Christ with mankind, or as Grétillat calls it, an expression of solidarity between Christ and men.

Grétillat is luminously clear about the priestly office of Christ so long as our Lord remained on earth. But he felt a difficulty about the continuance of that priestly office in heaven. He considered that the priestly office of Christ became extinct after the Passion and Resurrection because thereby the Redemption, Reparation, and Sacrifice on behalf of Humanity had been accomplished. Grétillat alludes to, but does not discuss S. Paul's declaration in Romans viii. 26 that the Spirit maketh intercession for the saints.

Accordingly Grétillat passes on to consider the Kingship of Christ. In this comes the Sending of the Spirit and the founding of the Church. The organs

The Older Protestantism in France

of the Kingship of Christ on earth are of two kinds: individual and corporate. The corporate organ of Christ on earth is the Church. The Church is a unique apparition in Humanity. A study of history convinced Grétillat that the distinction between the visible Church and the Church invisible which came to the front at the Epoch of the Reformation in the controversial interests of Protestantism against Catholicism, was not calculated to solve the problem. Grétillat is clear that the Church "replaces the visible person of Christ." But its ministry is a continuation of the prophetic office of the Old Covenant.

Coming to the subject of the Sacraments, Grétillat notes that the different conceptions of the value of a Sacrament may be grouped in two divisions: symbolical or realistic. The former regards the Rite only as a sign of something passed, present, or future; the other regards it as producing a real effect. Grétillat is a convinced believer in the realistic conception.

With regard to the Eucharist, the idea of Sacrifice was at an early date introduced into this Sacrament. It gradually became regarded as "a repetition of the sacrifice of Christ, made for the living and the dead." Grétillat, having rejected the heavenly intercession of Christ, could find no room for a sacrificial conception in the Eucharist on earth.

Whatever omissions or inadequacies are apparent from the Catholic standpoint in this remarkable French Evangelical exposition of the Christian principles, its adherence to the great distinctive doctrines of the Holy Trinity and the Incarnation is conspicuous.

III

A second example of older Protestantism is Adolphe Monod.* Adolphe Monod was a French Protestant leader whose Sermons were widely read in the second half of the nineteenth century. He taught very definitely much of the Evangelical Faith. He distinguished very clearly between the Word of God as an idea, or doctrine, and the Word of God as a personal reality. Jesus Christ is the personal Word, the Word Incarnate. The one is the expression of a thought, the other the actual presentation of Deity. To the criticism that Orthodox Christianity was exclusive, he replied that error is manifold but Truth is one. He acknowledged that the sixteenth century had shown itself prodigal in making affirmations of an absolute character, and that our age charitably reserves its affirmations to a small number of fundamental doctrines. Those doctrines might be condensed in two expressions: Jesus Christ and Grace. But that meant Jesus Christ adored as Divine Redeemer. And Grace meant the free gift of unmerited redemption. Unhappily however, complained Monod, this was far too extensive for many in the nineteenth century. They desired the Evangelicals to refrain from any definite affirmation of a

* *Third Series of Sermons*, 1881, vol. i, pp. 8, 9; vol. ii. p. 385.

The Older Protestantism in France

fundamental Faith. Monod replies that this desire was indefensible. Exclusiveness has been characteristic of the Protestant Church, of the Universal Church, of the Apostles, and of Jesus Christ Himself. The Apostles taught a quite uncompromising Religion. If an Angel from Heaven taught any other Gospel he was declared Anathema. Neither is there Salvation in any other. Christ Himself was just as exclusive. "No man cometh unto the Father but by Me." Christianity consists of absolute affirmations which exclude all contrary belief. To hold otherwise is not to hold a doctrine as Truth, but only as an opinion. And to do this is to deprive Religion of any driving force because it is destructive of any sense of reality. To be a Theist is to be exclusive, for it implies the negation of Atheism. Monod ridiculed the idea of the construction of a Church which left every member free to profess exactly what he liked.

Guizot,* whose appreciation for Adolphe Monod was great, says that Monod was dismissed from his functions as Pastor at Lyons on the ground that he was too exacting in his orthodoxy, and thereby a disturbing influence to the peace of the Church. He became Professor at Montauban, in 1836, and in 1847 was invited to become preacher in the Protestant Church in Paris. Guizot says that for Adolphe Monod faith in Christ as the Redeemer was supremely momentous, essential beyond words. It is this that makes the

* *Meditations*, p. 168.

very life of a Christian. The prevalent reduction of religious Truth to subjectivity was unspeakably deplorable and disastrous. The reproach of being exclusive he regarded as a commendation, for Truth is by its very nature exclusive. What deeply pained him was the request to substitute for the phrase—this is the Truth, the phrase—this is my opinion. While Monod acknowledged that the absolute dogmatism of the sixteenth century had carried the dogmatic principle to untenable extremes, yet there were certain fundamental Dogmas which to Christian Religion were absolutely indispensable. No man should be excluded from fellowship who relies upon the sole merits of Jesus Christ the Saviour and Lord of all.

The exclusiveness of Christian Religion was not concerned with persons, but with doctrines. Uncompromising definiteness is right when the object is to define the Faith which has been clearly revealed. But Adolphe Monod had no desire whatever to pronounce on the internal character of any man.

Guizot was deeply impressed by Monod's character. His piety was profound. His eloquence was of a high order. His impassioned earnestness of conviction could not fail to exercise great influence.

IV

One of the most attractive leaders in French Protestantism of a strictly orthodox type was unquestionably

The Older Protestantism in France

Frederic Godet.* He was tutor for a time to the Prince Imperial at Berlin, and afterwards preacher at Neuchatel. His commentary on S. John, which appeared in 1863, and was re-written in 1876, attracted very considerable attention in England as well as in France. Godet's exposition was written in a beautifully religious spirit and with full acquaintance with the German criticism of his time, and with profound recognition that the traditional faith concerning the Incarnation of the Eternal Son was what the fourth Evangelist taught in the opening verses of his account. If anything was clear as daylight to him, he said it was the authentic character of this incomparable, inimitable Book. There he found the self-conscience of Christ expressed. It was the life of God lived humanly. Jesus Christ is more than a human ideal. He is God giving Himself to man. If Christ is not something of God Himself, of the Divine essence, what has God given? In that case Christ has given Himself, but God has given nothing.

Godet's Conferences on the Christian Faith, given in 1869, exerted widespread influence. They were translated into English by Canon W. H. Lyttelton in 1881.† They include replies to Réville's reduction of the Resurrection appearances to mere visions; a very memorable Lecture on the Perfect Holiness of Jesus Christ, and another on the Divinity of Jesus

* *Life*, p. 327, by Philippe Godet, 1913.
† *Lectures on the Christian Faith*, p. 285.

Religious Thought in France

Christ. Godet replied with deep moral and religious earnestness to the criticism of Réville's *Histoire du Dogma de la Divinité de Jesus Christ*. The mutual equality of the Father and the Son expressed in S. Matthew xi. 27, impressed Godet profoundly. Still more that such claims could have been accepted by Jews. "There exist," said Godet, "in every Israelitish heart an innate horror of everything which tends to identify the creature with the Creator. And before the Apostles could have been brought to concede to their Master divine titles and attributes, they must have been driven to it by peremptory reasons, among which the only decisive one must have been the manner in which they heard Him express Himself respecting His person. Nothing external to this His testimony respecting Himself could have brought them to cross the limit which separates docility and admiration from adoration."

CHAPTER IV

The Newer Protestantism in France

THERE is a very wide and deep abyss between the Older Protestantism of France and that of the Newer Liberal Critical School, as represented by Auguste Sabatier.

According to Auguste Sabatier,* the Essence of Christianity does not consist in the revelation of supernatural Dogmas. He rejected the Incarnation. He thought that to regard Christ as the Second Person of the Eternal Trinity, consubstantial with the Father, removes Christ from History and transports Him into metaphysics. It makes Christ lose all reality, although he admits that the Church, at least in theory, maintains the Humanity of Christ alongside His Divinity. But in order to secure the identity of the Humanity with that of all other men Sabatier denied the Divinity. Sabatier quoted Strauss that "the Idea does not pour all its riches into a single individual. The Absolute does not descend into History." At the same time Sabatier was sure that it is needful to distinguish between the quantity and the quality, or rather the continuity of being. He admits that Christ was "without sin" and stood in an intimate relation with the Father, and in the relation of moral unity of love

* *Outline of a Philosophy of Religion.*

between God and man religious evolution is accomplished. Christianity therefore is the absolute and final religion of mankind.

Yet Christianity is for Sabatier pure individualism. In his opinion Christ promulgated no dogma, and founded no official institution. Neither in His language nor in His thought is there anything absolute. No doubt He accepted and shared the Messianic beliefs in which He had been trained like all the children of His race. Apostolic Messianism is Jewish and Catholic as much as Pagan. Protestants affirm that they belong to the Church because they belong to Christ. Catholics reverse the terms. Jesus did not admit the intervention of any external authority between the Father and the child. Sabatier resented a Visible Institution having divine authority, and held that thereby the autonomy of the individual conscience is compromised. Catholicism began under the unconscious action of pagan habits. Sabatier said that there is a radical opposition between the Catholic principle and the Protestant principle. In his opinion all compromises, all diplomatic negotiations will fail, because each of the two principles can only subsist by the negation of the other. The authority of the Bible is never separated in Protestantism from the right of the individual to interpret it freely. The antithesis between Protestantism and Catholicism became most conspicuous in the doctrine of the natural priesthood of all Christians as opposed to that of the super-

The Newer Protestantism in France

natural priesthood of a privileged clergy. "To speak of an immutable and infallible Dogma in Protestantism is nonsense. The decision of a Church cannot have more authority than that Church itself. No Protestant Church holds itself or can hold itself, without denying itself, infallible." He compares traditional Dogma to ice which melts in the warmth of knowledge and of piety. He attempts a triple division of the progress of Christianity. The Messianic form which was infancy, the Catholic form which is adolescence, and the Protestant form which is maturity. He explains that he is a Protestant, and thankful to be of Huguenot descent.

And yet in spite of rejecting the Catholic Conception of Dogma as immutable, Sabatier insisted that Dogma, meaning thereby doctrinal propositions which have become the object of faith, is a phenomena of social life without which a Church cannot exist. Dogma, previously compared to blocks of ice, is here compared to lava which once came burning-hot from an interior fire. The religious value of dogma is pronounced to be considerable, and without being either absolute or perfect in itself, absolutely necessary to the propagation and edification of the religious life. Dogmas must in the nature of things always be imperfect. Yet Sabatier was emphatically opposed to undogmatic Religion. By suppressing Christian Dogma you would suppress Christianity: by discarding all religious doctrine you would destroy religion. But Sabatier saw clearly that in breaking the authority of the Church, the Reformers broke up the basis on which the ancient dogmas had been built. But Dogma is open to criticism.

Auguste Sabatier's celebrated book on Religions of Authority and the Religion of the Spirit is a dexterous criticism alike of Catholicism and Protestantism as Religions of Authority. With remarkable skill he utilizes Protestantism against Catholicism, and Catholicism against Protestantism. While he rejects alike reliance on the Authority of the Church and reliance on the Authority of the Bible, he criticizes both these systems of Religion as members of the same family. They are both systems of Authority. He does not hesitate to contend that Catholics have the advantage because the Church as a social organism living and contemporary, has capacities to deal with actual problems of each age, which a Book, which is a document belonging to the past, cannot possibly rival. It is one thing to reason on the value of a book. It is another thing to compete with an Institution which has exerted an enormous empire for all the Christian centuries, and has rendered enormous service to humanity. Personally, of course, Sabatier regarded the dogmatic claims of Catholicism to be fiction and legend, but the Catholic Church is a political reality with which the powers of the modern world would have yet to reckon. Protestantism appears to Sabatier a fragile construction. There has been a progressive dissolution of dogma under the influence of biblical criticism. There have been compromises and surrenders. Rationalism

The Newer Protestantism in France

has won its victories. In the nineteenth century the Authority of the Bible decreased. Emotionalism has frequently taken the place of definite convictions. In France the Revolution brought down the Altar as well as the Throne.

In place of Religions of Authority, whether Catholic or Protestant, Auguste Sabatier endeavoured to establish the Religion of the Spirit. It is the Religion which consists of a life rather than of a Doctrine, and is produced in the individual by the influence of the Spirit. Sabatier attributes the founding of this sort of Religion to Jesus Christ. It is a Religion without priestly mediation. It is true that Jesus taught as one having authority, but the authority was not of an external nature. The authority of His utterances consists in their effectiveness. His method of teaching is the contrary to the method of Authority. Thus the Authority of Jesus is not the Authority of His Person, but only the Authority of His Teaching. Or if it is the Authority of His Person it is only so far as His person embodies His teaching. That ought to mean that the Gospel is in reality separable from the Person who was only its exponent. Sabatier asserts that the real object of faith is not the Man Jesus, but the Revelation of the Father in Him. The cult of Jesus, that is to say the separate worship of the Man Jesus, is, in Sabatier's opinion, downright idolatry. It is repugnant to Protestant piety. Jesus never demanded adoration of Himself. He aimed at creating the same

Religious Thought in France

filial relation between His disciples and God as existed in Himself. Sabatier ignores or glides over all sayings of Jesus implying difference between His relation to the Father and that of His disciples. Any such difference is characterized as metaphysical monopoly or religious egotism. Sabatier assumes that Our Father was the prayer which Christ Himself prayed, and not only the prayer which He taught to His disciples. Moreover the critic thinks that the Dogma which regards the Holy Spirit as a metaphysical entity has a paralysing effect on Christian life. No proof is given of this.

According to Sabatier, Christians are everyone for themselves Prophets, Priests, and Kings. And of course, when everyone is a King there are obviously no subjects. Every individual is his own Prophet and his own Priest. There is no external controlling authority whatever. Christianity is democratic to the very last degree. Absolute equality exists among the citizens of the Kingdom of God.

Sabatier, however, is too logical not to see that in that case, given this freedom of individualism, the problem must be faced how then can the Religion of the Spirit possess any definite contents whatever. Sabatier is more conscious of the difficulty than prepared for its solution. He recognizes that freedom must have a law. In Morals there must be such a thing as duty. There can be no liberty without it. Something similar is true in Religion. Freedom does not consist

The Newer Protestantism in France

in the absence of law, but in obedience to the law of our being. This, however, is not submission to something outside oneself: to rebel would be to strive against oneself. But the religious sentiment is for Sabatier essentially nothing else than conscious relation of a moral being to the law which rules it. This does not necessarily involve belief in God in the traditional sense of the word. Inward deference to the ideal of Humanity suffices. In which case the Religion of the Spirit possesses very little distinctively religious contents indeed.

However, the problem of the Person of Christ still haunted Sabatier. He returns again to what he admits is the central difficulty in the Religion of the Spirit. Does not the Person of Christ occupy the central place in His Gospel? Is it not presented to us as object of faith and of love? Is it possible to be a Christian without being attached to this Person by a definite and distinctive bond of attachment? Yet if this historical and external element is essential to Christianity, how can it be pure Religion, entirely inward and moral, the Religion of the Spirit? Sabatier confessed that he had nowhere found a clear and satisfactory solution of this problem. He finds that pious and learned men vacillate between the orthodox solution which makes the historic Person of Christ a metaphysical entity, a second God in the dogma of the Trinity, and the solution of unitarian rationalism which breaks every bond between this Person of Christ and the Christian

Religious Thought in France

Faith, and makes Jesus a prophet and a martyr to His own teaching. Others adopt a mediating position and content themselves with affirming the pre-existence of Jesus. Others indulge in pious expressions and cover their rationalism in a mystical cloud, but are unable to explain the attitude which Christ Himself adopts when He says to His disciples: Come unto Me, believe in Me, confess Me before men, love Me more than father and mother, follow Me.

Sabatier himself has in reality no solution to the problem which he realizes so acutely and represents so clearly. He can only reiterate that to believe in Christ is to identify oneself with His Words, and to appropriate His Teaching as a living principle. Sabatier takes refuge in the distinction which Ménégoz emphasized very forcibly between belief as an intellectual assent, and faith as a personal trust. Emphasis is laid on the generalities that life is anterior to thought and Religion to Theology. And Theology promotes or compromises Religion. Hence the importance of a sound Theology.

CHAPTER V

The Newer Protestantism on the Deity of Christ

FRENCH Protestantism teaching in the nineteenth century on the Person of Christ displays a gradual disappearance of belief in His Divinity, issuing in extreme cases in questioning His historic reality. This disappearance of faith may be seen in Albert Réville, Jean Réville, Ménégoz, and Auguste Sabatier. The extreme negative position is seen in Couchoud's work.

I

Albert Réville's *History of the Dogma of the Deity of Jesus Christ* was widely read in France, and was translated into English in 1878, the last Edition being in 1905. Réville begins by explaining that the doctrines of Religion are subject to the great law of natural development. He recognizes that the Dogma in question was until recently accepted universally except by a few Unitarian Protestants, and that it was generally supposed that no one could be a Christian who did not admit it. But Réville was convinced that there was nothing primitive in the Dogma, and consequently nothing essential to the very existence of Christianity. It is only one form among many others of the Christian faith. This information is given by way of introduction. After preliminary reflection of this nature, Reville approaches the really central inquiry: In what light did Jesus regard Himself? The answer, he says, is difficult. The great passage in S. Matthew xi. 27, is briefly dismissed in a note below the page, with the remark that it "strangely breaks the thread of the discourse, and resembles a rhythmical ecclesiastical formula." But it is admitted that the fundamental idea of this passage may be authentic. The fundamental idea being that "Jesus at the moment when he speaks, is conscious of being known properly only to God who reads his heart, while he alone thoroughly knows God as the Father." Réville thinks that "a different turn has been given under the influence of a subsequent theology." But he speaks with uncertainty. No adequate attempt is made to ascertain our Lord's self-consciousness, or to consider the implications involved in His use of the terms: the Father and the Son. On what must critically be considered as insufficient treatment, the conclusion is reached that "Jesus would clearly have repudiated every theory which attributed to him a superhuman origin."

Passing to consider the convictions of our Lord's followers about His Person, Réville lays stress on what he calls "their excited imaginations." They conceived Him seated at the right hand of God. They contemplated their Master as "Man become celestial." And although this was not the exact assertion of His

The Newer Protestantism on the Deity of Christ

Deity it was the beginning of the process of His deification.

The process went much further, Réville thinks, through the influence of S. Paul. Réville has much fault to find with the Apostle. He gave to the Person of Jesus an importance so absolute, so exclusive as the object of faith, that Christianity instead of remaining the religion which Jesus taught became the religion of which Jesus was Himself the object to Whom faith was directed. Christianity became Christ-centred. S. Paul laid great emphasis on knowing Christ after the Spirit rather than after the flesh. Christ was still human for S. Paul. "But nevertheless He is a Man Whose existence prior to his advent upon earth is taught with increasing clearness in proportion as the Pauline theology developed itself." The Pre-existence of Christ is expressly taught in Philippians, Ephesians, and Colossians. Réville is much impressed by the passage in 1 Corinthians viii. 6, "One God, the Father, of Whom are all things, and we unto Him; and one Lord, Jesus Christ, through Whom are all things, and we through Him." Whereupon Réville's comment is: "He was already so exalted many ages before He came upon earth, that we cannot conceive how He could rise still higher, unless He became equal with God." In Philippians ii, Réville rejects the idea that the form of God means equality with God, though he accepts the idea that the form of man means equality with man. He rejects it on the ground that Christ received as a reward for His self-renunciation, a title and privileges superior to those He had before. He does not inquire whether the exaltation is not attributed to the Son of Man. After tracing the Dogma of the Deity of Christ through the Patristic period, through Arianism, to Calvin, Spinoza, and Hegel, the conclusion ultimately stated is that "the Dogmas of the Trinity and the Incarnation, formed by Catholicism, modified by the Reformation, dissolved by the Socinian criticism, unacceptable to reason, and contradicted by history, have had their day, and the elements of truth which they contain must be clothed in other forms, and enter into a different conception of things." "For the God of the Trinity must be substituted the only God, above and within the world."

II

Jean Réville, Professor in the Protestant theological Faculty of the University of Paris, is a very clear exponent of what is called Liberal Protestantism. In lectures delivered in Geneva in 1902 he explained that Liberal Protestantism is essentially individualist. It is not a system of doctrines, but includes many varieties, and is therefore difficult to define. It maintains that religion does not consist in assent to a group of metaphysical dogmas, but in a disposition of the soul. It is strongly opposed to every intellectual servitude and to every Creed regarded as an obligation. The Refor-

The Newer Protestantism on the Deity of Christ

mers were extremely conservative with regard to Dogma. What Liberal Protestantism upholds is the authority of reason and conscience in the sphere of religion. Genuine Christianity is the Religion which Jesus taught, not the Religion which His disciples subsequently constructed about His Person and His Work. The letters of S. Paul, however admirable they may be, are only the Apostle's own speculations, nothing directly emanating from his Master. Jesus never ordered His disciples to believe in the Trinity, nor in any metaphysical doctrine about His Person, nor to accept any doctrines about the essence of Deity, nor to believe in His Resurrection, nor to submit themselves to a series of observances or devout practices, nor to celebrate religious rites, nor to obey any ecclesiastical authority whatsoever. And Liberal Protestantism adopts the same line. Religion, according to J. Réville, adapts itself to different theories about God. It is essentially the sense of a living relation between the human individual and the powers or power of which the Universe is the manifestation. Like Schleiermacher, Réville regards Religion as a consciousness of dependence, although this consciousness is not by itself sufficient to create religious life. From the varieties of the phenomena of nature reflection arrives at a supreme principle of Unity, and bestows on One Deity the adoration which he had previously distributed among many gods. This most fundamental of all conceivable Dogmas—the intelligence and self-consciousness of the Ultimate Reality behind the Universe—is assumed with a somewhat startling superficiality, and without any apparent consciousness that in comparison with that stupendous Dogma all other Dogmas are immeasurably easier of belief. Man however, so it is said, never ceases to possess the assurance that the Supreme Being, the principle of the Universe, is living. And reflection is said to confirm his intuition. And in whatever manner men conceive of Deity there is no Religion without a living God. Doctrines professed by Jesus and by His Apostles have long ago vanished. What remains as the proper basis of the Gospel of Christ is specifically religious, independent of doctrine, morals, sacraments, and institutions, summarized as the Fatherhood of God and the Brotherhood of man. Réville owns that this Liberal Protestantism is often characterized as an impoverished Christianity. But in his opinion it is the Gospel of Christ. The doctrine of Redemption by the Sacrifice of Christ is rejected by Liberal Protestantism, as it rejects the Dogmas of the Trinity and the Metaphysical Divinity of Christ, for the same reason. They are not rational, nor are they the Religion of Jesus. Redemption by the Sacrifice of Christ is in Réville's opinion excluded by the Parable of the Prodigal Son.

At the same time Réville insists on the peculiar power which Christianity possesses. He asks what Religion has shown with more constraining power the supreme grandeur of sacrifice? But he does not pause

The Newer Protestantism on the Deity of Christ

to explain what the secret of this appealing influence is, nor to inquire whether that secret does not consist precisely in the doctrines which Liberal Protestantism rejects. He thinks that in the Dogma of Redemption the Church has transferred to the Man-God the adoration and the love which naturally react against the Father sacrificing the Son. Réville insists that the Liberal Protestant must not allow himself by mystical influence to transfer to the human Christ the worship and adoration which are due to God alone. The Adoration of Christ is in Réville's opinion an intrusion of Greek paganism into primitive Christianity, and a denial of the Monotheism of the Gospel.

Réville is conscious that Liberal Protestantism in virtue of its individualism renders corporate agreement and co-operation more difficult. He inquires pathetically, How is liberty to maintain itself within the Church if Liberals are indifferent to social religious life and confine themselves within their individualism. At the same time he insists that Religion is not to be identified with the Supernatural. He laments the disconcerting fact of reaction towards the Catholic Church of many a Freethinker. Men who revolted into complete irreligion are found returning to the Mass and entrusting the education of their children to representatives of the ancient orthodox tradition. He reminds his readers that Liberal Protestantism does definitely believe in a Future Life, and closes his reflections with the hope of a future in which all Dogmas, Sacraments, and Rites which have perpetually divided men, will disappear.

III

Ménégoz, in a study on the Doctrine of the Trinity, quoted the orthodox belief, and went on to say that for him it is hardly possible, with his modern philosophical and psychological conception, to admit that three personal consciousnesses can form a single individual. Consequently he set that doctrine aside. The writers of the New Testament were all of them Monotheists. Their Deity was the Jehovah of the Old Testament. Ménégoz held as indisputable that the Doctrine of the Trinity could not be found in the New Testament in the shape of dogmatic instruction. He raised the question whether the doctrine is implicitly there. That resolved itself into two inquiries: First, whether the New Testament taught the essential Divinity of Jesus Christ; and secondly, whether it taught the personality of the Holy Spirit. Taking this second inquiry first, Ménégoz gave it as the result of his reading that the New Testament personifies the Spirit but does not represent the Spirit as a person. The other inquiry about the Divinity of Jesus Christ Ménégoz considered more complicated. He did not think that in the Synoptic Gospels Jesus is called the Son of God otherwise than in a Messianic sense. No New Testament writer identified Him with Jehovah. The idea of an Incarnation of Jehovah is absolutely

The Newer Protestantism on the Deity of Christ

foreign to the sacred writers. After His Resurrection His disciples gave Him royal homage. And when this was transferred into regions of Greek and Roman polytheism, where Kings and heroes were readily divinized, it is not surprising that a similar process took place in the case of the Divinity of Christ. In the subjective imagination, the Father and the Holy Spirit are two distinct Beings. But this subjective imagination must not be transferred to objective realities in Deity. That, in Ménégoz's opinion, is where the Fathers of the Church went astray. Such procedures dissolve the Divine Unity. Ménégoz acknowledges that the Union of God and Man in Christ has certainly a metaphysical foundation. In fact we cannot conceive it otherwise. But Revelation is Moral and Religious. In that order Jesus Christ is the Word of God, that is to say the perfect Revelation of Truth. If the question is raised whether the knowledge of God which results from the Immanence of the Spirit of God in the Spirit of Man is not a metaphysical knowledge, Ménégoz replies that the question leaves him quite indifferent. Religion is a personal relation between God and man, and this personal relation was realized perfectly in Jesus Christ. Jesus lived with God in the most intimate faith and love, confidence and veneration, submission and devotion. Hence He merited the title Son of God *par excellence*: Father and Son represented a moral relationship, not a metaphysical.

Thus the Trinity according to Ménégoz is resolved

into the following theory: The Father is the transcendent Deity; the Son is God immanent in Humanity, revealing Himself in History and fully in Jesus Christ; the Spirit is God indwelling in the individual and rendering within us witness to our spirit. More briefly still: the Father is God transcendent, the Son is God objectively immanent, and the Spirit is God subjectively immanent.

Ménégoz is well aware that this theory will be adversely criticized as nothing else than resuscitated Sabellianism. All that Ménégoz can reply to this is that Sabellianism held a theory of chronologically successive manifestation of the Divine, whereas he himself holds that the manifestations are simultaneous.

IV

Sabatier's book about S. Paul displays complete familiarity with the negative conclusions of such German critics as Zeller as to the historic value for example of the Acts of the Apostles. But Sabatier's book also displays an independent judgment, and a refusal to be unduly influenced by such opinions as that S. Luke was indifferent to historical accuracy and careless of self-contradiction. Sabatier is convinced that if the discrepancies in the three accounts of S. Paul's conversion had never existed "those who will not admit the miracle would just as decisively reject the testimony of the Acts of the Apostles." Zeller, however,

The Newer Protestantism on the Deity of Christ

frankly owned that the denial of the miraculous rests on a philosophical theory, and that theory lies outside the scope of historical research.

Sabatier was convinced of the objective reality of the manifestation to S. Paul outside Damascus Gate. S. Paul's adhesion to the Gospel was, above everything else, the complete negation of his previous life. When Sabatier arrives at S. Paul's account of our Lord's original state, the passage in the Philippian Epistle about being in the form of God, the French writer is deeply impressed by what he calls "the most exalted metaphysical definition ever given by S. Paul to the Person of Christ." He is sure that the words "express a substantial relation to God." But yet he cannot bring himself to believe that the expression "in the form of God" means absolute Divinity. He thinks that there is still beyond what S. Paul describes as the form of God, "a higher position still which Christ might have thought of seizing but which He did not usurp." Sabatier passes without reflection over the astounding idea that a Palestinian Jew should have been content not to aspire to equality with God, or that Saul of Tarsus should have commended a fellow-Jew for not usurping a yet higher relation to God than that of being in the form of God. How such claims, limited indeed by acknowledgment of something yet required to constitute identity with Deity on the part of a Man, could ever have been made or commended in the Nation sensitive beyond any other to the slightest infringement of the prerogatives of Deity, Sabatier does not even consider. His theory is that "Christ is of the Divine nature. But there is this difference between Him and God: that what He will become eventually He has yet to become; and He will become this actually, by the full development of His moral being."

Thus, to put it briefly, Christ was potentially Divine from the first, and this by a process of development He actually became. This would mean that in Christ we contemplate the evolution of Deity. The series of propositions which Sabatier expounds appear to be that Christ is of the Divine Nature, He is not God, He is potentially Divine, He becomes Divine at the consummation of His Development. Sabatier recognizes that the humiliation of Christ requires that there should be renunciation on His part. What then did He renounce? It was certainly necessary that Christ should have been already, in Himself and by nature, of a higher condition. In other words, He pre-existed. Christ therefore seems represented as originally a supernatural Being belonging to the heavenly sphere who by an act of renunciation descended to the experience of life under human conditions. Sabatier's conception of Christ is therefore a modernized Arianism. But what moral merit there was in such a Being declining to usurp the characteristic of Deity is not explained, and indeed is not susceptible of explanation.

The Newer Protestantism on the Deity of Christ

Sabatier's view of Christian development is that it has taken two separate lines, the one *idealist*, concerned with metaphysical conceptions, the other *realist*, concerned with the natural and embodied. The former is concerned with Truths which are of all times and places, and commend themselves to intelligence in virtue of their own reasonableness. From this standpoint Christ may be the Teacher of universal ideas, but His person can no more be indispensable to His Religion than the person of Plato to the system of philosophy which he taught. But the consequence of this separation of Christ from Christianity is that the Christian Religion ceases to be positive and becomes abstract and theoretical. The latter—the realist—starts with history, but makes Christ the second person of the eternal Trinity consubstantial with the Father. There it advances from history into metaphysics. But to supernaturalize History in this manner is to destroy it. The Dogma transcends the contingent and the human and the limitations therein involved in Jesus Christ. Consequently His life loses all reality. We have no longer a Man before our eyes, although the Church theoretically maintains His humanity beside His Divinity. But the Divinity absorbs the Humanity. Sabatier thinks that traditional Christianity is incurably docetic. The Kenosis theory illustrates this in his opinion. Sabatier accepts the criticism of Strauss that the ideal can never be realized in all its richness in any individual. The Absolute does not enter History.

Either Christianity detaches itself from the Person of Christ, or else it will cease to be the ideal Religion of Humanity.

Sabatier admits that Strauss's criticism is in a sense quite true. But that it depends on a quantitative estimate of perfection. It is obvious that the perfection of knowledge, including all scientific discoveries and all the degrees of civilized progress and all the forms of human life cannot possibly be found at any one period in history. No individual, however great, could exhaust all the varieties of human experience. But this quantitative estimate is a mistaken one. The greatness of Christ is not in *quantity* of experiences, but in the *quality* of them. It lies in the moral and religious instincts of His being. The perfection of Christ lies in His relation with Deity.

Sabatier sees that the perfection of Christ as the ideal human life consists in His sense of Sonship with God. What Sabatier calls the filial relation with the paternal.

Unhappily it is here that Sabatier parts company with the Faith of Christendom. He is unable to see that Christ's consciousness of Sonship to the Father, while undoubtedly it does involve the relationship within human limits, goes beyond those limits and includes a consciousness of an eternal relationship between the Father and the Son. Sabatier is content to leave subtleties to the theologians. But that only evades and does not face the problem how the self-

The Newer Protestantism on the Deity of Christ

consciousness of Christ permitted Him to affirm or imply what transcends the rights or reason of any created personality.

Sabatier complains that a Christ exalted to these metaphysical elevations of identity with the Divine is thereby separated by an insuperable abyss from mankind. This incommunicable privilege of Jesus isolates Him from all the rest of the race, whose origin is entirely terrestrial. His experience is not and can never be mine. But Sabatier entirely fails to realize that in this reduction of Christ to the levels of the creature He is thereby deprived of His power to raise humanity. The dogma of His Divinity is precisely the source and explanation of His strength.

Pathetically enough Sabatier takes refuge in the historic Figure from which the attributes of Divinity have been removed.

Accordingly, Sabatier bids us study the religious attitude of Jesus alike towards nature and towards mankind. Nature is the Will of His Father to be accepted with joy and confidence. For the Father directed all things.

It is true, reflects Sabatier, that Jesus had not the ideas about the Universe which for the last three centuries science has imparted to ourselves. His horizon had not the immensity of ours. He doubtless shared the cosmological conceptions of His time. His universe was relatively narrow and small. He had never, like Pascal, felt overwhelmed by the eternal silence of boundless space. Though why not one hardly can conceive, remembering the Psalmist's words.

He had not that formidable apprehension of the inviolable laws of nature, nor the obscurities of human origin, in the far-off dawn of civilization.

All those limitations, says Sabatier, must be freely acknowledged. But the filial piety of Jesus did not depend on His knowledge or His ignorance. This is a sphere which the more or less of culture does not affect. Irreligion was not less easy nor less frequent in His time than in ours. It is an illusion to suppose that, if the Universe was less extensive, it was less full of scandalous failures, or of difficulties for the moral life, or less arduous for piety or for faith. Filial piety was the solution of all its problems—the ideal is "Father, into Thy hands I commend my spirit."

The individual confronted with the Universe and its laws has still before him the necessity of self-renunciation. The sacrifice must either be at the altar of a blind Deity called the nature of things, or else of a heavenly Father. The Religion of Jesus, which is the latter, is the religion of hope.

v

In the year 1924 there appeared in Paris a little book with the title, *Le Mystère de Jésus*. So far as the title goes it might have been a little manual of devotion

The Newer Protestantism on the Deity of Christ

and spiritual meditation. It was in fact extremely otherwise. Couchoud, its author, had been studying the attempts of the rationalistic critics to account for the Person of Jesus within the limits of the purely natural. *Historical criticism*, starting on the assumption that the supernatural is to be rigorously excluded, found itself confronted with two facts: In the first place the origin of the Christian movement was due to the action of a Galilean Jew. In the second place, the movement which he originated speedily deified its originator. The rational criticism reduced Jesus of Nazareth strictly within the limits of the human, and ascribed His deification to the exaggerated enthusiasm of His followers.

That was briefly the conclusion at which this school of advanced criticism arrived. It was the explanation in which Strauss and Renan and Loisy, with due allowance for their diversities of outlook, substantially agreed. Renan was prepared to assign to Jesus a privileged position at the head of the human race. Loisy regarded Him as a Person of obscure origin who was mysteriously deified. This explanation Couchoud was unable to accept. Couchoud replies that this explanation fails to do justice to considerable elements in the problem, and is to himself as an unbeliever quite incredible.

It is incredible for the following reason. To say that Jesus of Nazareth is a man whom His followers deified bristles with incredibilities because, says Couchoud, it involves the assertion that Saul the Rabbi deified a fellow-Jew.

If the great Religion of the West is essentially merely the deification of a man, then in spite of its immense diffusion, it is of a type inferior both to Judaism and to Islam, both of which have guarded themselves most carefully against any corresponding invasion of the prerogatives of Deity.

As an example of contrast with these negative criticisms of the Newer Protestantism on the Deity of our Lord may be set the work of a Catholic Theologian—Lepin, Professor at the great Seminary at Lyon.*

Professor Lepin has given a summary of Couchoud's books. He assembles in condensed form the main estimate which S. Paul has formed of the Person of our Lord. S. Paul can say that in Him dwelleth all the fulness of the godhead bodily; declares that no man can say that Jesus is the Lord but by the Holy Spirit; applies to Jesus the term Lord, which is the ordinary Greek rendering of the name of the God of Israel. If Israel says that "to the Eternal God every knee shall bow" (Isa. xlv. 23), S. Paul says that "at the name of Jesus every knee shall bow" (Phil. ii). If Zechariah saith that "the Lord my God shall come, and all the saints with thee" (Zech. xiv. 5), S. Paul

---

* *Le Christ Jesus*. Son existence historique et sa divinite, par M. Lepin, Professeur au grand seminaire de Lyon. Bloud et Gay. Paris. 1929.

The Newer Protestantism on the Deity of Christ

speaks of "the coming of our Lord Jesus Christ with all His saints" (1 Thess. iii. 13).

Loisy who thinks that while the conception which S. Paul presents of Jesus as the Lord and the Son of God is full of obscurities, all the precautions of his language did not prevent the dogma of the Divinity of Christ being advanced through the worship of the Lord Christ. His judgment is that S. Paul, by sanctioning this apotheosis of Jesus has inflicted on the transcendent monotheism of Israel the gravest injury that it was possible to inflict.

But Loisy's critical insight does not permit him to cast the reproach of deifying Jesus exclusively on Saul of Tarsus. It was not the inference of an individual. It was the religious sentiment of the mass of believers which made Christ to be the Lord. And the worship of the Lord Jesus preceded the primitive Christology.

What Couchoud feels is that while critics like Strauss think it easy to attribute the apotheosis of Jesus to the enthusiasm of His followers, it is quite impossible to do so for the simple reason that they were Jews. Whence came this religious sentiment applied to a Jew who had recently died upon a Cross? No doubt, says Couchoud, it is true that men have been sometimes deified. In certain localities that was possible. But there was one nation in which this process was utterly impossible. That nation was Israel. The Jew adored Jehovah, the only God, the transcendent Deity, whose very name they did not venture to pronounce, who was parted by unfathomable depths from every creature. To associate a Man with Deity was a sacrilege, an abomination of the deepest dye. A Jew would have been martyred rather than set a man in perilous proximity to the prerogatives of the unapproachable Deity. And that a Jew, a Hebrew of the Hebrews, a Rabbi, a Pharisee, should ever have done this—that is a thing of all things most incredible. That a Jew should do this of another Jew, his own contemporary: such thing could not happen, no, not in the Dispersion. There is no example of it. There were other aspirants to the office of Messiah. Not one of them was awarded the attributes of the transcendent Deity. The case of Jesus is unique. Now for the historian unique cases are invariably enigmas.

Such is the general drift of Couchoud's reflections. What then will he infer? If we expect the conclusion to be that this amazing ascription of Divine prerogatives can only be accounted for by the reality of our Lord's equality with God, we shall be mistaken. Couchoud has already warned us that he does not believe. The Christian conception of the Incarnation of God in human flesh is to him unthinkable. The *modern mind* is unable to appreciate a Personality Who is at home in two worlds. The doctrine is dismissed. Why? On the ground that it is "a pre-Kantian conception." At the same time it cannot be denied that it has been adopted by great minds. Augustine, for example, and S. Thomas and Pascal. But in the

The Newer Protestantism on the Deity of Christ

twentieth century we cannot appropriate it. Of course a God-man would account for everything. But the modern mind cannot accept this.

But then neither can Couchoud accept the Human Jesus. For the figure creates insoluble enigmas. What then is the solution? Couchoud's solution is that this Gospel figure simply never existed at all. He is a creation of the minds of believers. He is nothing more than an object of faith. That is to say, an illusion.

Lepin has not much difficulty in showing that neither Strauss, nor Renan, nor Loisy support that conclusion. They are all convinced of the reality of the existence of the Man Jesus of Nazareth.

Couchoud does not appear to see that his solution becomes even more inexplicable than the deifying of a Figure who existed only in imagination. The dilemma to which he feels himself reduced, either to deny the historic existence of Jesus or else to acknowledge His Divinity, should at any rate suggest the wisdom of reconsidering whether after all the mystery of Jesus is not explained by the impression of a Divine personality on His contemporaries. The Problems of religious History are not really to be solved by denying their reality.

But it is most instructive to find this acute modern French writer totally unable to accept the theory of the rationalist critics that Jesus was an exceptional man whom His adherents deified. Couchoud sees how utterly impossible it is that strict Unitarians like the

Jews, stern Monotheism, with the conviction that God is one only Person deeply ingrained into their very constitution, could ever have consented to deify a Man. And yet they did it. There is no adequate explanation of these facts except that Jesus is actually more Divine than Human, and that the ascendancy of His Divine personality forced others to a recognition of His Deity, in spite of their Unitarian Tradition, and led to an enlarged conception of the Being of Deity which was impossible until Jesus came.

The truth is that Jesus cannot be accounted for by a historical criticism which limits history within the sphere of the merely human and natural. If the supernatural is ruled out Jesus Christ cannot be explained. It is only when the supernatural is acknowledged that His claims and His influence and the interpretation placed upon Him become intelligible.

CHAPTER VI

The Newer Protestantism on Redemption

As illustrations of the change which has passed over modern French Protestantism on the doctrine of Redemption which, of all others, is at the very heart of Evangelical Christianity, reference should be made to Eugene Ménégoz and Wilfred Monod, and the reflections and criticisms of Gaston Frommel.

I

Eugene Ménégoz, Professor in the Faculty of Protestant Theology in Paris, well known among other works for his exposition of the Epistle to the Hebrews, illustrates very clearly indeed the departure of Evangelicalism in France from the Orthodox doctrine of such a leader as Godet. Ménégoz devoted great attention to the question what is it in which Salvation really consists. He drew the sharpest distinction between faith as assent of the mind to intellectual propositions, and faith as surrender of the heart to God. The former he called belief: to the latter he confined the term faith. Belief in a dogma or fact, however true either might be, had no saving effectiveness. Salvation depended on the soul. Accordingly he represented his position by the formula—Salvation by faith independently of beliefs. He who dedicates his soul to God is saved independently of his beliefs. He resented the Orthodox conception, which in his opinion imposed on the human conscience a burden too heavy for it to bear. He carried the principle of Individualism to the extreme conclusion that every separate Congregation and person had the right to discriminate independently of the rest. Faith in Jesus Christ was not indispensable. It was possible to dedicate oneself to God and be saved independently of belief in Jesus Christ. Indeed, the author faced the ultimate inquiry, are we not constrained to say that belief in the existence of God is indispensable to Salvation, for how can a man dedicate his heart to a God in whose existence he does not believe? Ménégoz admits that the objection is logical. But he thinks exceptions possible. Unconscious belief may develop into a conscious belief. It should be added that for Ménégoz Father, Son, and Holy Spirit are but triple manifestations of Deity, different shades in the manifestation of the Divine to the world.

In Ménégoz's version of Christianity the Apostolic doctrine of Redemption disappears, and also the Divinity of our Lord. The modern theologian is in Ménégoz's opinion compelled to subject the Epistles of S. Paul to a process of interpretation similar to that which the Apostle inflicted on the teaching of the Old Testament Prophets. The author does not find the doubtfulness of S. Thomas was for the more con-

The Newer Protestantism on Redemption

firmation of the Faith. His reflection is that if the assurance of S. Peter did not convince S. Thomas, it is possible that the assurance of S. Thomas may not convince ourselves.

Ménégoz's well-known treatment of the sacrificial conception of the Death of Christ in the Epistle to the Hebrews is characteristic of his entire outlook. He lays stress on the fact that the idea of ritual sacrifice is absolutely foreign to Protestant Christianity, which does not celebrate the Sacrifice of the Mass. He thus rejects the principles of a sacrifice of reparation offered by Christ to the Father. On the great subject of the Sinlessness of Christ, he observes that the Gospels record no trace of sin in the Self-consciousness of Jesus, and that all His followers firmly believed in His perfect sanctity. On this basis he explains the Passion as illustrating the unmerited sufferings of the righteous in a sinful world. The righteous organically united with the unrighteous expiates their sins according to the Law of Solidarity. There, he says, you have the truth about Christ's Death. Beyond that we cannot go. He does not attempt to solve the fact that the Apostles go very far indeed beyond that. Nor does he seem conscious that there is no Gospel whatever in such an explanation. He compares Christ to a shepherd defending his sheep against the wolves and dying in the process. He quotes, however, but does not accept the Pauline explanation that Christ's Death was an offering and a sacrifice to God.

Religious Thought in France

As for the Divinity of Christ, that is to say in the strict sense of the word as Deity, Ménégoz is unable to find it in the Epistle to the Hebrews or in S. Paul. This momentous conception is very superficially treated. It is acknowledged that the Son of God is a superior being, He pre-existed, He is the firstborn of creation. But there was no Incarnation of Deity. Apparently the Arians were the Orthodox exponents of S. Paul, and Athanasius a great perverter of the truth. Thus Ménégoz agrees with the older Unitarians in a position which the modern Unitarians are unable to retain.

Ménégoz discovered that his theory of Salvation by faith independently of beliefs provoked considerable opposition among French Protestants. He says that it scandalized a number of theologians in the Protestant world. He did his best to reassure his co-religionists by further explanations. His theory, to which he gave the name of *Fidéisme*, was Scriptural; far remote from the intellectualism of ancient orthodoxy, and also from the moralism of the modern liberal school. He acknowledged that his formula was liable to misconception, but he was compelled to maintain it. He owned that true doctrines produce a salutary effect and that false doctrines exert an injurious influence, in the whole range of life whether social or individual. He owned, moreover, that faith implies belief. But he held that the saving value does not reside in the belief but only in the faith. Yet he was constrained to admit, apparently

The Newer Protestantism on Redemption

under controversial pressure, that it was the knowledge of the Truth which saved men. And yet of course it was possible to have the knowledge without allowing it to influence the heart. In which case, however valuable the Truth might be and was, it did not save.

When these explanations had been given it might seem eminently desirable that since true doctrines were acknowledged to produce a saving effect, the doctrines dismissed as false might fairly be reconsidered. For it cannot be denied that if they were true their effectiveness would be extremely great; and therefore whether after all the Author might himself have been mistaken, and the Church of the Ages gifted with truer insight, made the subject of further and prolonged reflection.

Distinction exists between the subjective condition of Salvation and the objective instructive means by which saving faith is produced. Doctrines certainly exert a very powerful influence on the mind, emotions, and will. But they do not necessarily prove productive of faith. That is why Ménégoz described saving faith as being independent of beliefs. At the same time knowledge of the Truth is an objective condition of Salvation. When then Ménégoz was accused of holding a theory of Salvation by sincerity he complained that he had been misunderstood. Whether the phrase—Saved by faith independently of beliefs—is false or true depends on the sense given to the term independent. The faith which saves is, however, explained to be faith in God. Being asked whether saving faith was consistent with disbelief that such a person as Christ ever existed, Ménégoz replied that he doubted whether any man could be found who denied the existence of Christ. But if a man with such an opinion could be found, Ménégoz suggested that he will discover his error in Paradise, and would fall at the feet of Christ as S. Thomas did when he realized his ignorance in face of the Risen Lord.

II

Wilfred Monod illustrates the change which was passing over French Protestantism at the beginning of the twentieth century.* In his exposition of the Death of Christ he distinguishes first the Priestly Interpretation expressed in sacrificial terminology. "According to certain apostolic assertions, the Crucifixion was the means of Reconciliation between humanity and God." Jesus Himself is acknowledged to have spoken of the Blood of the Covenant, and of blood shed for the remission of sins. But Monod thought it doubtful how far the disciples of Christ are bound by similar symbolism in explaining His death. "Jesus the layman," says Monod, "belonged to the line of the Prophets."

A second view of the Death of Christ is the Prophetic Interpretation. "So persecuted they the Prophets which were before you." The Passion is explained on the

* *The Road to God*, 1928.

The Newer Protestantism on Redemption

principle that the better a man is the more he is bound to suffer in such a world as this. Consequently the best will suffer most. The misdeeds of the guilty fall upon the innocent. But what Gospel is contained in this interpretation is left unexplained.

A third interpretation of the Death of Christ is called the Christian. It is maintained that Christ did not die in order that God should pardon, but because God pardons.

III

Gaston Frommel, Professor of Protestant Theology at Geneva, was remarkable for the religious fervour with which he held that the real distinction of Christianity was that in it God did not primarily intervene to instruct, but to save. He taught his students that Christianity is essentially a religion of Redemption.* He went much further. He gave his students an account of his own conversion from worldliness to Christ. He told them that it was as they might well believe a sweet yet painful thing to open his heart to them with the frankness that he had done. This was in 1895.

Frommel deeply impressed upon his students the Sinless Perfection of Christ. He taught that in Jesus Christ alone God has revealed the plenitude of His character. He dwelt on the arresting uniqueness of the great utterance—"Be of good cheer, I have overcome the world": audacious assertion on the lips of Him

* *Etudes Morales et Religieuses*, 1907, p. 62.

whom the world would crucify, and apparently overcome, yet who became "the only legitimate object of human faith." He drew out with admirable force and clearness the vital distinction between knowing Christ according to the flesh, and knowing Him according to the Spirit. Criticizing the state of religion in the nineteenth century among French-speaking people, Frommel complained that if the theology of his time had made considerable progress it had paid dearly for that progress by many defects. It had re-discovered Jesus of Nazareth, but it risked the loss of Christ the Saviour. Historical works which the nineteenth century began and the twentieth century continues, enable us to penetrate better than any previous time into the earthly career of the Son of Mary. His humanity is fully described. The sublimity of His character attractively displayed. But the Son of Man conceals from us the Son of God, and the spiritual value and the redemptive power of the Evangelical account escapes us.

The sympathy of the present day is much more with Jesus of Nazareth than with Jesus Christ. An ethical conception vaguely associated with the merciful Fatherhood of God suffices for the piety of many believers, and the Christian Religion is reduced for many among them to reverence for a beneficent Deity whose gracious message is imparted in incomparable words by the perfect man. Our theology is the Humanity of Jesus, and scarcely attains to His Divinity. Frommel stressed

The Newer Protestantism on Redemption

the urgent need of a recovery of the doctrine of Reconciliation. He realized keenly that Divine forgiveness was not an easy thing. The Moral indignation in a Being who is absolutely pure was in his conception of the Christian Revelation a profound reality. Frommel urged with much earnestness the inadequacy of human repentance. It was invariably inadequate. Hence he was led to appreciate the Apostolic Doctrine of Redemptive Sacrifice.

CHAPTER VII

The Newer Protestantism on the Nature of the Church

A CHARACTERISTIC exposition of the idea of the Church as held by the Protestantism of the newer type is to be found in Edmond Scherer's *Essay on the Church*. Scherer was certainly one of the ablest critical thinkers in French Protestantism about the middle of the nineteenth century. His intellectual career began in Orthodox Protestantism and gradually descended to indefiniteness, closing ultimately in the loss of religious faith. The following criticisms belong to the middle period of his evolution.

Scherer contended that the Church is not one of the constitutive elements of Christianity. Consequently he declined to trace the idea of the Church as taught in Scripture. Yet he defines the Church as the Society of Christians. Union with Christ results necessarily in union of Christians. But his conception of Union is that there is no Church with an external organization expressing and maintaining unity. The Church divides itself into fractions corresponding to the subdivision of particular truths, or following the difference of nationality and other natural obstacles, to say nothing of sin and error. Thus there are only Churches. There is no one Church, no organic form. The Church is

The Newer Protestantism on the Nature of the Church

only an abstraction representing the Churches as if they were a unity. This ecclesiastical manifestation is imperfect, but yet necessary. The diversity of the Churches appears to Scherer quite consistent with essential unity of the Church.

Christians are not to be regarded as purely individualists, but as constituting a Body. It is tempting at first sight to identify the Kingdom of Heaven with the Church. But the identification he thinks is mistaken. The Kingdom of God is more abstract, the Church more concrete. The former is a Dispensation, the latter an Institution. And yet he notes that two passages in S. Matthew (xvi. 18, xviii. 17) include the idea of the Church. But he is doubtful of the value of the text. In the teaching of the Apostles the idea of the Kingdom of God retires before that of the Church, which is contrary to what we find in the Teaching of Christ.

Organization and Spirituality are presented in their actions and reactions, but the value of the Organization to the Spirituality is not really appreciated. Schism is described as a reaction against exclusive objectivity, and against the Sacramental idea. It is a revolt of the religious conscience against the actual Church which Catholicism misrepresents. It wants the actual to be the ideal. But it aspires to the impossible.

Thus to Scherer the spirituality of the Church involves that its unity is invisible. Spiritual unity is not adequately expressed by organization. The outward is in this way conceived in opposition to the inward. The spiritual is invisible. It is contrasted with the material. The ecclesiastical tendency has been to identify the external Church with the mystical Church. The mystical tendency lays the stress on the invisible and spiritual.

Christian development is the history of the conflict between these two tendencies—the spiritual and the material. Catholicism is institutional, sacramental, episcopal, hierarchical, organ of ecclesiastical unity. This system did not impose itself without reactions, which Scherer proceeds to trace in the usual manner. The Catholic system is in his opinion religious materialism in its completest expression. It wrongs the Spirit by the multiplicity of its institutions. Hence Protestantism. The Reformation was, he thinks, a return to evangelical principles with regard to the nature of the Church.

Scherer, however, is clear that the Anglican belief is an exception. Alone among all the official utterances of the Reformation Anglicans define the Church exclusively on its visible side. Whereas Calvinism treats the Church invisible as being that which the Apostles' Creed represents—Anglicanism is concerned about the Visible Church.

The significance of the revolution wrought by the Reformation on the idea of the Church consists, according to Scherer, not only in the distinction between the Visible Church and the Invisible, but rather in the pre-eminent importance assigned to the invisible.

The Newer Protestantism on the Nature of the Church

Thus the Protestant conception of the Invisible Church produces the logical conclusion that the Visible Church is, of course, a necessary manifestation, but also inadequate, that the form which the Church assumes will not be one, but many. There will be various types of Organization, tendencies towards systems. The various forms are not arbitrary, but the development of various portions of the Truth. The vital principle is everything. The organization changeable. The soul is essential, the body is secondary. Life expresses itself in variety, different species, and individualities more or less pronounced. It is the natural result of the imperfection of all ecclesiastical expression that these expressions should be numerous, that their value is purely relative, none of them represent the truth entire. There is no form of Christianity possessing absolute right, no consecrated type.

Nevertheless the fact remains that this question whether there is or is not a particular ministry with the authority of a Divine Institution not only divides the Roman Church from the Churches of the Reformation, but also divides these latter from each other. He refers to the "Eglise Anglicane." Scherer proceeds, of course, to identify himself with the negation of any divinely chosen ministry. The usual congregationalist conception follows. Each congregation has absolute power to organize itself, and to govern itself without any control from without. The minister is essentially a preacher of the Word. Apostolic succession is pronounced a fiction. The Apostolate was essentially personal and temporary.

Edmond Scherer realized to a degree quite unusual in a foreigner the distinctive characteristics of the English Church. He saw that the Reformation in England differed greatly from the Reformation elsewhere. The changes wrought by Henry VIII by no means resembled the revolutions which occurred in Europe elsewhere. The English Reformation profoundly modified the religious practices of the Nation and extended itself to doctrine as well. But the English innovations displayed less desire to make a clean sweep of the past than that which animated the Continental Reformers. There were in fact two contrasted tendencies. The conservative-minded reverenced and loved the ancient forms of religion. They were prepared to modify, but not to destroy. They broke with the Papacy under the pretext that it had become unfaithful to primitive tradition. But they had no intention to break with Tradition. Contrasted with this conservative school of thought was another whose inclinations were revolutionary. They cared very little for the work of centuries. They clung to an ideal as to constitution and doctrine which they imagined they had discovered in Holy Scripture. These radicals of the Reformation thought they could not make wide enough or deep enough the abyss which ought to separate the new Christian Society from that from which it parted. The Conservatives were the Anglicans

The Newer Protestantism on the Nature of the Church

proper, the revolutionary party were the Puritans. The result was that the Episcopal Church was the product of these antagonistic tendencies. The traditional tendency is shown in the sacerdotal, catholic character, in the institution of the Episcopal, in the forms of worship, in the Liturgy. The innovating tendency is expressed in the Thirty-nine Articles. The co-existence within one Communion of these opposing tendencies has had its advantages, but it has been the cause of permanent agitation. Scherer proceeds to trace the well known perpetual reactions which have marked the history of the English Church ever since the Reformation.

Scherer's estimate of our National character is instructive. Englishmen, he says, are not gifted with critical faculties, but they are gifted with an energetic power of reason, and a certain intellectual right-mindedness which helps them to overcome prejudices to which they are more naturally disposed than other nations.

The fundamental difference between Catholicism and Protestantism is that the former represents Christianity as historically expressed across the centuries, whereas the latter derives direct from Scripture. Scripture is for Protestantism the only source of religious knowledge, the only rule of faith. Thus the ordinary creed of Protestantism contains one article alone—belief in the Bible. Both types of Christianity carry their principles to its ultimate extreme, the one attributes infallibility to the Church, the other to the Bible.

Scherer went on to show the effects of the critical spirit on the fundamental belief of Protestantism. Protestantism set Scripture in the place which Tradition assigned to the Church. Protestant theology in the seventeenth century was immeasurably more subservient to the letter of Scripture than either Luther or Calvin had ever been. Protestants thought they could not go too far in their cult of the Bible. The effect of Biblical criticism on such estimate of Scripture was devastating. Protestantism having exaggerated the authority of the Sacred Book found itself faced with a crisis which threatened its very existence.

Protestantism in France, says Scherer, was just as badly smitten by modern criticism as any other country. The modern movement affected Protestantism more seriously than Catholicism, for obvious reasons. Scherer, with engaging impartiality, confesses frankly that there is something which is alike more human and more divine, something grander and more living, something more congenial to thought and more attractive to imagination, in the conception of a vast institution invigorated by the Spirit from above, and under the influence of that Spirit, developing in accordance with the needs of mankind—there is something in all this grander and truer than a doctrine which confines the Spirit of God within the limits of a letter.

The question which Scherer's critical instincts pro-

The Newer Protestantism on the Nature of the Church

voked was whether Protestantism would survive, or did it possess the capacity to change. Catholicism could not, he thought, greatly change. It had added indeed in the nineteenth century a fresh dogma to its Creed. Scherer must mean the dogma of the Immaculate Conception. For he was writing in 1861. And in any case he was convinced that Catholicism without infallibility would no longer be Catholicism. Protestantism, on the contrary, cannot aspire to Infallibility. It has no interpretation of the Gospel which is final. Protestants exercise the right to call in question the gravest traditional beliefs, to revoke doctrines formerly admitted, to examine everything afresh. Scripture is no longer for Protestantism an infallible authority.

Consequently, in Scherer's opinion, writing as a French Protestant, it is not merely Protestantism which is in danger; it is Christianity, it is Religion. Religions which really live are the Religions which possess a Church, sacred Rites, and definite Dogmas. The real significance of Dogmas is that they are replies to the great ultimate problems which have always haunted the spirit of man. They concern the origin of the world, the atonement of evil, the destiny of mankind. Dogmas such as these imply a Revelation. The Christian Religion is of necessity the history of a Divine intervention in the destiny of the human race. It is the record of acts by which God created and saved the world. It is either this, or it is nothing. It follows that Religion contains elements which are other than

Religious Thought in France

religious sentiment. They are historic elements, or they are dogmatic.

And here Scherer advances an acute reminder that Religious sentiment itself may come into conflict with these elements of Religion. So long as some Authority in Religion prevails the faithful accepts the Religion as something already made. But where the Religion of Authority is overthrown the individual man is left to make his own selection among religious ideas and principles. He retains only those doctrines which appeal to his personal intelligence or emotions, and give satisfaction to his individual religious needs. In this way religious sentiment becomes the determiner of religious truth. The individual accepts congenial elements of doctrine, but rejects what he regards as purely speculative. He wants his religion to be altogether religious, confined to piety and appealing to his heart. He eliminates from his belief dogmas which in his opinion do not seem conducive to that result.

Scherer's comment on this outcome of Protestant individualism is instructive. Being himself of Protestant antecedents he acknowledges that this gradual emancipation of faith makes a strong appeal. It certainly looks like a natural process, a means by which religion and critical conclusions may be harmonized. It might be thought that by this selective method the religious sentiment could solve the difficulties which dogmas present to the modern mind, and that the Religion of the Future might consist in a kind of rationalized

The Newer Protestantism on the Nature of the Church

Christianity or Christianized rationalism, which without excluding religious fervour would leave to critical thought its perfect liberty.

To Protestant individualism the idea is most attractive. Scherer owns that this is so. Yet the prospect of leaving the religious sentiment of the individual to determine what Dogmas the Religion of the Future shall contain fills him with profound uneasiness. Is Christian rationalism really a Religion? When the positive Dogmas of Christianity have been eliminated, what is left but a lifeless corpse? Can Christianity, when reduced to a shadow, possess any invigorating force? Does it not closely resemble Deism and share the same meagreness and sterility? Does not the power of the religion reside precisely in those Dogmatic formulas and supernatural legends? Can genuine piety survive the destruction of these metaphysical principles? Are not the very elements which religious sentiment desires to separate from Religion essential to the preservation of Religion in the actual difficulties of social life? When criticism overthrows the supernatural as useless and dogma as irrational; when the religious sentiment on the one side, and the demands of an exacting reason on the other, invade belief, and in the process of assimilating it, completely change its character; when no religious authority any longer prevails, beyond the personal consciousness of each separate individual; when a man, after penetrating all mysteries, confronts the Deity to whom he aspires;

is he not liable to reach the conclusion that the Deity is nothing else than Man himself, being only the conscience and the reason of man personified? And will not religion, under the pretext of becoming more religious, be found to have passed out of existence altogether?

The Newer Protestant conception of the Church's nature, a conception which carried independence to extremes, and subordinated the contents of the corporate Faith to individual decision, was strongly resisted by Protestants who adhered to the older belief. But the tendency has been in the contrary direction.

CHAPTER VIII

The Issues of Modernism in France

IT is not the purpose of these pages to relate once more the story of Modernism and the course of Biblical criticism of a negative character in France. That has been done in many other places. Yet it is not possible to omit from a study of religious thought in France during the nineteenth century some account of the effect which criticism of Scripture has sometimes exerted on the religious outlook of the critic. There is, of course, no more conspicuous example of this effort than is seen in the career of that most distinguished critic, Alfred Loisy.

The three large volumes of Loisy's autobiography, reaching a sum total of 1,700 pages, are much more than the record of an individual career. They contain the completest account we possess of the controversy on Biblical criticism and the Modernist Movement in France. The materials from which the author has made selections were very extensive, but the work would have been improved by condensing. There is much unconscious self-revealing. And whether regarded as a study of the relations between criticism and faith, or of the gradual disappearance of personal religion, these volumes awaken many serious reflections.

As Professor at the Catholic Institute in Paris under

the presidency of Mgr. d'Hulst, Loisy was associated with Duchesne, whom he criticizes severely, and with Vigouroux, Secretary of the Biblical Commission, writer of some twenty volumes of eminently safe, indeed ultra-conservative, studies on Scripture. Loisy as a critic was very soon in trouble with the authorities. His independent treatment of Biblical inspiration caused so much alarm that Icard, Head of the College of S. Sulpice, forbade his students to attend the Lectures. In a chapter appropriately entitled "Publications and Tribulations," Loisy recounts that his opinions on the date of the Proverbs of Solomon were denounced at Rome, with the result that he was unofficially informed that the injury which his opinions inflicted on the literary glory of the Hebrew King was resented in high places, and that if he continued on these lines he would not escape an official condemnation. In spite of the warning he started a periodical of his own, *L'Enseignement biblique*, intended for the instruction of young priests. Whereupon d'Hulst expressed the hope that the periodical would not become dangerous to its editor. Meantime Loisy confided to his private diary the reflection that the Church at the present hour was an obstruction to the intellectual development of mankind. Not that this obscurantist influence is necessarily involved in its principles and constitution, but is an abuse which easily springs from them. Loisy assures his readers that he had not yet begun to doubt the essential presuppositions of

The Issues of Modernism in France

Catholic Theology. Yet he did not shrink from inditing painful sentences about the sacred legend of Judaism and Christianity, which Duchesne and he, in spite of real or verbal precautions, were labouring to demolish in the interests of Truth.

Further complications arose. d'Hulst, the principal, was sympathetic towards the modern critical school and anxious to mediate between the conservative and progressive extremes. His biographer, Baudrillart, recorded years ago how greatly d'Hulst appreciated Loisy's learning and ability, but he was in a difficult position, and naturally apprehensive about the safety of the Institute. Yet he wanted to be fair to those on the rationalist side. Prompted by conciliatory motives he published in the *Correspondant* of 1892 an Essay on Renan. It was shortly after Renan's death. d'Hulst declares quite uncompromisingly that Renan's philosophical presuppositions had determined his critical conclusions, and that he had outraged the religion recognized by the State; but at the same time d'Hulst admitted that the instruction given in the theological Seminaries had been elementary and obsolete. This was followed by another Article on the Biblical Question, well meant as an overture for larger toleration, but producing in orthodox circles precisely the contrary effect. In acknowledging the existence of errors in the Bible, d'Hulst risked his own condemnation. There was a storm of opposition. Rome was disturbed. d'Hulst felt obliged to make a pilgrimage and explain in person to the Pope the motives which prompted his essays. He returned to Paris convinced that if he hoped to avert a public censure he must guarantee the suspected orthodoxy of the Catholic Institute. He was forced most reluctantly to inform Loisy that it was impossible to retain him.

This, however, was the time selected by Loisy for publishing in his periodical an Article on the Inspiration of Scripture, criticizing the view that divine inspiration necessitates the absolute truth of the inspired word. He declared that non-Catholic critics of the Bible had arrived at a certain number of conclusions which in all probability they would never surrender, since they had powerful reasons for regarding them as scientifically verified. Loisy's article put d'Hulst in despair. Cardinal Richard was aghast. A Meeting of Bishops in Paris decided that Loisy must be dismissed. He resigned his professorship.

Towards the close of the same year, 1893, Leo XIII issued his Encyclical, *Providentissimus Deus*. It affirmed that no error is compatible with Divine inspiration. Loisy contended that Divine Authorship is not applicable to a book. Cardinal Richard advised him to suppress his periodical, which after an interval he did. He also wrote a letter to Leo XIII professing his entire submission to the doctrine of the Encyclical on the study of Holy Scripture. If he expressed himself publicly in the usual deferential terms he could not resist observing privately that he was not an adept in

The Issues of Modernism in France

the art of genuflection. Cardinal Rampolla's reply was to the effect that the Pope had received Loisy's letter with special favour, but advised that the writer should apply his talents to cultivate more particularly some other branch of science. The exasperated recipient of this reply exclaimed, did the Pope and his Secretary of State imagine that you can change your special scientific study as easily as you change your shirt. The sequel was that Cardinal Richard made Loisy Chaplain of a Convent School for girls. There he remained five years.

As to the state of his religious convictions, he says that he did not accept literally any article of the Catholic Creed unless it was, "Crucified under Pontius Pilate." He seems to have regarded Religion with singular detachment as an immense force which had dominated the history of mankind in the past and seemed destined to dominate it in the future. But of personal Religion very little is revealed.

Loisy ceased for a while to publish anything in his own name. But he wrote anonymously over various signatures: such as Fermin, or Jacques Simon, a somewhat fantastic blend of Bossuet's Christian name with the surname of his well-known critical opponent. Anonymity, however, did not shield his writings from official condemnation. The long established Journal to which he contributed, the *Revue du Clergé Français*, now unhappily deceased, received a letter from the Cardinal Archbishop of Paris condemning Loisy's

Article on the Religion of Israel, and forbidding the publication of the remainder.

The fate of Loisy's most celebrated book, *L'Evangile et L'Eglise*, is from any point of view pathetic. Written to prove that Harnack's reduction of the Essence of Christianity to the solitary doctrine of the Fatherhood of God, could not on Harnack's own premises be sustained, Loisy's book was irresistible. His proof that the Doctrine of the Kingdom of God was essential to the Teaching of Christ was conclusive.

But the sensation created by this little red book was immense. Troeltsch appreciated it. von Hügel was deeply sympathetic. Robert Dell said, "to many of us who are Roman Catholics it seems that M. Loisy has found at least the main lines of a synthesis between faith and criticism." Batiffol criticized it with great severity. Dr. Inge, then Dean of S. Paul's, said that "no intelligent reader can fail to see that M. Loisy's attitude towards the Gospel history is that of rationalism pure and simple. In his *Le Quatrième Evangile*, supernatural events are simply set aside as unhistorical; and the same presupposition seems to underlie the argument of his two other books." Cardinal Richard condemned *L'Evangile et L'Eglise*, as seriously disturbing the faithful or fundamental dogmas of Catholic learning, especially the authority of Scripture and Tradition, the Divinity of Jesus Christ, etc. In 1903 the Congregation of the Holy Office condemned five works of Loisy and placed them on the Index.

The Issues of Modernism in France

Cardinal Merry del Val, Papal Secretary of State, sent a letter to Cardinal Archbishop of Paris, which the latter read to Loisy, requiring immediate and unreserved withdrawal of the five volumes. Loisy informed the Archbishop that this demand was impossible for him to comply with. The Archbishop himself insisted that he must retire to a religious house in order to recover a Catholic mentality. This condition appeared to Loisy ludicrous.

Loisy wrote to Pius X declaring his desire to live and die in the Communion of the Catholic Church. He had no wish to contribute to the ruin of the faith in his native land. It was not within his power to efface in himself the results of his studies. But so far as concerned himself he submitted himself to the judgment pronounced against his writings by the Congregation of the Holy Office. As a proof of his goodwill to promote peace, he was ready to relinquish his teaching in Paris and to suspend the publication of the scientific works which he had been preparing.

Loisy's religious creed went to pieces. He said: "von Hügel believes altogether differently from myself on the divinity of Jesus Christ. Setting metaphysical verbal controversy aside, I no more believe in the divinity of Jesus Christ than does Harnack or Réville. I regard personal incarnation of God as philosophic mythology. Christ holds less place in my religion than in that of Liberal Protestants. For I do not attach so much importance as they do to this revelation of the

Religious Thought in France

Fatherhood of God. If I have anything in religion, it is rather pantheist, positivist, humanitarian, than Christian. I do not attribute to the essence of the Gospel that absolute and abiding value which Harnack desires to recognize in it."

Two years later (1906) Loisy wrote a letter explaining his attitude to Religion, in which he said that the fundamental religious problem of the present time was not whether the Pope was infallible, or whether there were errors in the Bible, or even whether Christ is God, or whether there is a revelation. All these problems are superannuated or they have changed their meaning, and depend on the one and only great problem whether the Universe is soulless, and consciousness of man finds nothing more real, more true than itself. He concluded with the reflection that faith demands Theism, but reason tends to Pantheism.

In a further letter he repeats von Hügel's opinion that reason leads to monism, but the heart is able to find God. But for himself Loisy cannot find Him. God is for him an ideal projection of human intelligence.

The Encyclical, *Pascendi Dominici Gregis*, of 1907 led to Loisy's exclusion from the Roman Communion. Cardinal Merry del Val, Papal Secretary of State, required him to condemn unreservedly all and each of the propositions condemned by the decree, *Lamentabile*; and the Modernism condemned by Pius X in the Encyclical, *Pascendi*. Loisy replied to this that the decree *Lamentabile* contained various

The Issues of Modernism in France

extracts from his writings, but with their meaning gravely misrepresented. He could repudiate these, protesting against the meaning imparted to them. Other extracts seemed to him indisputably true, and it was impossible for him to pronounce them to be false. He was unable to live in the intellectual atmosphere of the decree *Lamentabile* and the Encyclical *Pascendi*. The Cardinal reiterated his demand, requiring submission within ten days. Loisy refused and there followed in 1908 his excommunication. He says that the announcement brought him a feeling of genuine relief.

These volumes are by no means concerned only with Biblical criticism. They are concerned with the purpose of the Ultimate Reality of Religion itself. The author does not confine himself to historical criticism. He introduces his own speculative theories and philosophic presuppositions. He goes far beyond the province which he has made his own, into a province much deeper and in which there is no reason to credit him with expert capacity or experience. The formidable fact confronts us in these volumes that one after another the advanced critics lose all faith in supernatural religion, and indeed in the personality of God. Margival begins as a priest agreeing with Richard Simon, ends as a layman engaged in a firm of publishers. Marcel Hebert similarly begins as a priest, and throws aside his orders and terminates his career in a vague philosophy of which even Loisy himself confesses its unsatisfactoriness.

Religious Thought in France

When we reflect on the existence of great Theistic Religions independent of Christianity, there is plainly no reason why Biblical criticism, however advanced or individualist, should end in denial of the personality of God. Are there no grounds in the Natural Universe, and in the intelligent and moral and spiritual capacities of man, to suggest a contrary conclusion? Have not millions rested their interpretation of life on these?

Loisy's strenuous indictment of the baleful influence of authoritative restriction on the freedom of the historical critic is powerful, and indeed effective. But at the same time the total loss of anything that can be called Religion goes far to neutralize his accusation. He seems entirely and strangely unconscious that his negative conclusions provoke reaction towards Religion. Biblical Criticism is not necessarily ruinous to faith, nor can criticism ever be an adequate substitute for Religion.

No notice of these volumes could reasonably omit a reference to Loisy's friendship with von Hügel, a friendship extending over more than thirty years. It is superfluous to dwell on von Hügel's sympathy with Loisy's critical labours, or on the encouragements which he lavished on the French professor's troubles, or on the efforts which he made in the highest quarters to secure considerate treatment for his friend. Yet it is impossible not to feel that the difference between them was profound. von Hügel watched with grave concern

The Issues of Modernism in France

the diminishing hold of Loisy on anything that can be called Religion. In an impressive, indeed pathetic, letter von Hügel sees that the line which Loisy is taking will, if pursued, lead to fuller expositions of his sceptical conclusions. Such a result von Hügel owned would be very painful and very harmful to many souls. Yet he had no fear that life's experience would not ultimately lead our fellow-mortals beyond the realm of radical scepticism. To von Hügel Loisy was the born enemy of the Transcendent, while the Baron took the Transcendent under his protection—not, however, that it needed it. Loisy's influence on Religion has become increasingly negative, whereas von Hügel's last work was to bequeath to mankind his convictions on the Reality of God.

The most important of the eminent French critic's later works is the volume called *La Naissance du Christianisme*, published in 1933.* In his autobiographical Memoirs as has been already seen, while relating the History of Modernism in France, Loisy has also revealed the gradual disappearance of his own belief in Christ, or in the Supernatural.

It is therefore no surprise whatever that his latest literary production carries destructive criticism to its natural conclusions. It is true that many of the criticisms contained in this new book the author has made before.

* Alfred Loisy, *La Naissance du Christianisme*, Emile Nourry, Paris, 1933, 36 francs.

But they are here accumulated and condensed and re-expressed with a fresh incisiveness and with a more decisive air of finality. It is also true that there was far more reliance on the Gospel accounts and far more assurance in *L'Evangile et L'Eglise* that we possessed the actual utterances of Christ than is to be found in the author's latest book. He is not at all prepared to follow such extremists as those who deny that the central Figure of the Christian Religion ever existed. Loisy's historic sense recoils from the opinions of his fellow-countryman Couchoud, expressed in *Le Mystère de Jesus*. Couchoud persuaded himself that a pre-Christian dream about a Suffering Deity was transformed into a living religion by the imagination of S. Peter. Loisy is convinced that it is quite impossible to account for the Christian Religion in the absence of the Person in whom it originated. But while such negative theories are dismissed as incredible, destructive criticism of the historical value of the Gospels is carried out by Loisy so extensively that comparatively little of any solid worth is permitted to remain.

What is bound to impress any reader of Loisy's latest book is the remarkable frequency with which such words as fiction, legend, vision, recur. Page after page these words are encountered and reiterated. Thus the Stories of the Nativity are pronounced to belong to the order of mythical fiction. The substance of the teaching in S. Matthew is pronounced only to repre-

The Issues of Modernism in France

sent the Legend of Jesus. What does not come from S. Mark in S. Luke is pronounced "legendary fiction and mythical construction." The book of the Acts is even worse. The missionary preaching of S. Paul is "mythical fiction and legend"; "artificially composed." It is pronounced incredible that S. John Baptist should have discredited his own baptism as merely symbolical. "Little frauds" of this kind are said to be significant. The relation between John Baptist and Jesus reported by the Evangelists is pronounced to be a legend. We are to reconcile ourselves to know only that in the time when Pontius Pilate was procurator of Judaea, a prophet arose in Galilee in the region of Capernaum. It is asserted that Jesus did not wish to found a Religion and never dreamt of doing so. The promise that the Apostles would sit on thrones judging the Twelve Tribes of Israel is said to have been probably not uttered by Christ, but invented by the first Christian Community in honour of the Twelve. At the same time Loisy is convinced that Jesus is not presented in the Gospel to His contemporaries as a moralist, nor as a mere prophet, but as an ambassador of God. As to the treachery of Judas, Loisy pronounces it difficult to say what reality corresponded with this incident. The foresight attributed to Christ is set aside as dramatization and the work of an apologist. So we find a note on "the legend of Judas." Loisy is quite certain that the Crucifixion was a solid fact. But whether there was an accusation before the Sanhedrim is pronounced uncertain, and not very probable. Barabbas is pronounced a fiction, introduced to transfer from Pilate to the Jews the responsibility of the Condemnation. The burial by Joseph of Arimathæa is another legend. Indeed, Loisy is sure that on the day when Jesus died, not a soul could have foreseen the incomparable future which awaited "the unfortunate prophet of Nazareth." Whatever prospects may have been hoped for Him received on Calvary the most complete and crushing refutation. Loisy himself affirms all this.

Moreover Loisy is perfectly clear what sort of Figure it is that the Evangelists proclaim as the object of their faith. It is by no means a merely human Figure. It is not even the very greatest that ever lived. It is unmistakably a Divine Being whom the Evangelists represent, endowed with Redemptive attributes which are His and His alone. Loisy describes the primitive belief about this mysterious personality. How His adherents came to declare that Christ is the proof of the Love of God for man, and that Christ died for the Redemption of the sinful human race. How this "mythology," as Loisy calls it, seemed to promote a deep and courageous faith. How it enabled them to face difficulties and to overcome torments and persecutions. How they were convinced that Christ is the Son of God, and by His origin and His Nature as Son was the reflection of the Deity, superior to the Angels, and that through His agency the worlds were created,

The Issues of Modernism in France

and that He is the eternal Priest of Humanity with the Father. Moreover that, although Christ appeared in the Flesh, He did not originate in Humanity. In fact, in Him dwelt all the pleroma of the eternal Deity. Loisy thinks that in the New Testament Christ is represented as not usurping equality with God, yet He is represented as pre-existing in the form of God, and He is proclaimed as Lord, sharing in the Name and the Power and the Glory of Deity. Loisy is himself moved from his habitual coldness, and becomes subdued by the sublimity of the marvellous conception of the Christ presented in the opening phrases of the Fourth Evangelist.

Now the singularity of all this lies in the contrast which Loisy has drawn between "the unfortunate prophet" about whom so little can with any certainty be known, and the stupendous interpretation of His Personality, with all its marvellous sublimity, which Loisy acknowledges that the New Testament writers proclaim about Him. Loisy can only attribute this entire mighty fabric to the unlimited power of faith. Religious faith, in his opinion, is nothing else than the effort of the mind and imagination and the will to break through the apparently mechanical and fatal limitations of existence. Thus belief in the Resurrection was spontaneous. Faith overcomes all the stubborn reality of facts. Peter was principally responsible for this. His faith became infectious. Back in Galilee he had a vision during days filled with recollection of his vanished Master. He induced his former companions to see it as he did himself. And these humble people, in the simplicity of their hearts, persuaded themselves that Jesus not only lived but reigned in the glory of the Father.

It is significant that in spite of all his negations Loisy is entirely convinced that the Person whom the first Christian preachers proclaimed, and in whom the Evangelists believed, was by no means a merely human Figure, but supernatural and exalted at least to the closest intimacy with Deity. Loisy is certain that the Human Jesus of Liberal Protestantism is not the Christ of the Apostolic Religion. The Scriptural central Figure is not simply the Son of Man, He is the Son of God in a sense which at least no other can ever share. This perception of the unhistorical character of a Christ within human limits is impressive coming from a critic of so negative a kind.

It has been very naturally remarked by the editor of the *Hibbert Journal*, and the remark is all the more impressive coming from so independent a thinker, that after reading Loisy's account "it would seem at first sight that no connection could exist between the astounding development of the Christian Mystery and the brief career of the Galilean prophet." No wonder that some, despairing of finding a point of contact between things so disparate, go further than M. Loisy and take the final step which he refuses to take, by denying that such a person ever existed. "No wonder that others, after rejecting miracles elsewhere, find a place for it here."*

When we reflect on Loisy's latest work we are, of course, in the presence of a critic of exceptional ability and reputation, who has spent a life in reaching these negative destructive conclusions. But it is impossible not to feel that even from a purely critical standpoint there is something strangely subjective and individualistic in this superabundant, unsubstantiated ascription of the words and works of Christ to legend, fiction, fraud, and imagination. It is impossible to forget that over and over again Loisy's assertions would be contradicted by other critics of very high distinction. There could be no greater delusion than to suppose that these extremist assertions are matters on which modern criticism is agreed. It is exactly the contrary that is the case. Undoubtedly we shall find alike in Germany and in France eminent critics repudiating much that Loisy has asserted. Individualism largely pervades this whole book. And we cannot forget it. Moreover, Loisy writes from the standpoint of an agnostic, of one who lives apparently without any personal experience of religion. And it may reasonably be asserted that critical penetration into the value of the religious experience of other human beings requires some spiritual qualification on the part of the critic. It may be quite unconsciously, but surely it is inevitable that the absence of any personal experience

* *Hibbert Journal*, 1934, p. 341.

of religion must affect the critic's capacity for weighing and estimating aright the religious experience of his fellows. The unmusical is not usually considered the competent critic of the musician. Is the non-religious the competent determiner of the value of the Christian Revelation?

CHAPTER IX

The Future of Religion

PROPHECIES on the disappearance of Religion were published in France towards the close of the nineteenth century, as well as in other lands. Guyau's *Irreligion of the Future*, written from an agnostic standpoint, was in its ninth edition in 1904. It is a work of remarkable independence, adversely criticizing all forms of Religion alike, Comtist as well as any other, on which it has many severe things to say. Protestantism is regarded as an untenable half-way house, an assent to certain supernatural propositions, qualified by an illegal refusal to accept the implications. Pascal is commended for criticizing, with the logical spirit characteristic of the French, a Protestant's unbelief in the Eucharist. If Jesus Christ is God, what difficulty is there about it?

On Liberal Protestant interpretation of the Scriptures Guyau considered that it read back into the text conceptions which are purely modern, and by that process made them a reproduction of nineteenth century ideas. Thus the literal is reduced to the figurative, and the Liberal Protestant acknowledges that there is undoubtedly in Jesus something Divine, but are we not all of us divine in some way or other? Why be surprised that there is a mystery about Jesus when we are a mystery to ourselves? Thus Christ loses His Divinity: or rather shares it with all the Angels and all the Saints. Thus everything becomes figurative except God. But, asks Guyau, Why should the Liberal interpretation pause there? Freedom of thought has yet another step to take. And then God becomes, like the rest, a figure of speech—a popular personification of the ideal. And saved by the self-sacrifice of Another becomes changed into saved by our own exertions.

Guyau notes that Liberal Protestants were not numerous in France, and those who had seceded from Orthodox Catholicism did not venture to abandon Christianity. But this type of Christianity maintains that if Jesus is nothing more than Man, He is at least the most extraordinary of men. He has by an intuition which is at once natural and divine discovered the supreme truth on which humanity must live. He was in advance of His age. He did not only speak to His own century, but to all the centuries, and we cannot replace Him. On this interpretation Guyau reflects that this Liberal Protestantism is certainly a theory which deserves to be discussed, but it has no special distinction from the numerous philosophic sects which in the course of history have desired to attribute to one who was only human an authority greater than that of man.

Guyau further reflected that for many Positivists Auguste Comte was a sort of Christ of somewhat more recent date, and who had not the good fortune to die

The Future of Religion

upon a Cross. Guyau went on to deny that a man of genius can be the expression of all the ages, or escape from being more or less the expression of his own particular age. Guyau could not allow the humanitarian Jesus the position which Liberal Protestantism endeavoured to retain for him. Guyau entirely rejected the Catholic conception of Incarnation and Redemption, but he declined the compromise of a Christ who was not Divine and yet exalted into a superhuman elevation.

Guyau was not able to understand Asceticism, nor what he calls the obsession of sin.

On the momentous question, whether the religious sentiment is innate and imperishable in humanity, he criticizes the opinion of Taine and other Frenchmen that Religion is intellectually unfounded and emotionally indispensable. This attitude is characterized as eminently superior and somewhat disdainful. Guyau rejected the idea that the religious sentiment is innate, and asserted that the perpetuity of religion had never yet been proved. He could not see why the dissolution of Religion should involve the dissolution of popular morality. Guizot, however, regarded Christian Religion as indispensable. Guyau laid stress on the case of criminals who were habitually religious.

Guyau was strongly averse to religious education given by a priest. As an agnostic he regarded it as an infringement of the liberty of thought. Yet he did not see how religious education was to disappear, at any

Religious Thought in France

rate all at once. After all it was not so bad a thing that fifty-five thousand persons in France should be or appear to be occupied in other than material interests. And it was good that some men should pursue an ideal of disinterestedness above their powers, while so many pursued aims inferior to their powers. What was needed was that priests should receive an education superior to that which was being given them. He contemplated country priests occupied in the study of botany, mineralogy, and music. The priest is not to be destroyed, but to have his spirit transfigured and given other occupations than the mechanical recital of his Breviary. Guyau was also of opinion that if the History of Religions were introduced into the Schools of the State it ought to deal chiefly with what does not concern the History of the Jews. It should give the morals of Confucius, Greek mythology, and Indian Religion.

Adverting to Religion in the home, Guyau deals with the question whether a Father ought to have a Religion, if not for himself yet for his wife and his children. If his wife has a Religion ought he to leave to her the education of his children? Guyau replies that a Father's duty is to make his own convictions triumph in his own family. He ought not to conceal his own convictions. Sooner or later they are bound to become known.

Guyau himself confessed that the most interesting of the problems of education is how to speak to a

The Future of Religion

child concerning death and human destiny. He shrinks from informing a nervous child when its Mother died that it would never see its Mother any more. A materialist would be wrong to make positive affirmations about matters on which we can have no more than probabilities. Truth is not of equal value at every stage of life. And there is such a thing as subjective immortality, that is to say survival of the departed in the memory of the living. So other people have argued, but the critic is not satisfied. Yet he has no real solution to offer. Turning to the case where the Father is a Freethinker and the Mother a Catholic, it is advised that the Father should inform the child—this is my own belief, and these are my reasons for it. Perhaps I may be mistaken. Your Mother thinks otherwise, and she also has her reasons, good or bad for her belief. In which case the child at any rate may learn toleration.

Guyau treats with considerable frankness and some apprehension the problem of the increase of population under the influence of Religion and without it. The force of the injunction—increase and multiply, has been very widespread and great. The Jewish influence was very strongly indeed in that direction. Stress is laid on the fact that distinguished men, perhaps two-thirds of them, belong to large families. An only son appears to have less chance of becoming a remarkable man. Parental indulgences tend to weaken his moral exertions. The first-born are often the less

Religious Thought in France

vigorous or the less intelligent. Maternity perfects itself in reiteration. Like poets and artists, it is unusual for a Mother to produce her masterpiece first.

It is possible for a nation to disappear from lack of children. Guyau is disquieted over the actual state of France in this respect. It economizes in children. It is only Catholics, Protestants, and Jews who maintain a certain reproduction of race in France. Those who act conscientiously and religiously in this matter are a negligible quantity. To five children born in England there were only three in France. Statistics have been produced to show that the members of the Institute of France have as a rule only one or two children. Similar small families abound among the artisans. In the middle classes it is unusual to find a family with more than one or two children. Now it requires at least two to replace in the next generation their parents, and a margin must be added to allow for the unmarried and the sterile. The middle-class restriction means national suicide: the depopulation of France. Lax morality shows in this matter a culpable neglect. Thus the alternative appears to be either a return to traditional religions, or gradual extinction of the race.

These reflections lead Guyau to attack the Catholic restriction to celibacy, whether in the priesthood or in the Monastic orders. With a singular absence of impartiality he sets over against the childless priesthood the distinguished sons of Protestant ministers,

The Future of Religion

without taking into any account the intellectual benefits which the Monastic Orders have conferred upon the world in their great theologians. But he has been already constrained to recognize that Catholicism has exerted powerful influence in encouraging the direction —increase and multiply.

The dominant motives for the restriction of the family are as a general rule economic. It is strange, reflects Guyau, that this should be in France where paternal and maternal love is more tender than in other countries.

The conclusion reached is that the relation of religious beliefs with the maintenance of the race becomes a momentous problem. Neither Morals nor Politics have undertaken seriously to supply the place of Religion in this matter.

After satisfying himself that the close of nineteenth century had witnessed the dissolution of Dogma and of religious morals, Guyau speculated whether there will be a Revival of Religion or not. In his opinion such a Revival could only happen by a unification of existing Religions, or else by the emergence of a new Religion. The former alternative, dismissed on the ground of their incompatibility, is very superficially treated. The latter alternative is regarded as more than doubtful, partly because prophetic personalities appear to be extinct. This great profession has expired. Nobody dreams of aiming at it any longer. Moreover a new Religion would indispensably require a new idea.

Religious Thought in France

Recent attempts to found a new Religion are destitute of any new ideas. Comtism, for example, retains nothing of Religion beyond its external Rites. It is an endeavour to maintain life in a body from which the heart has been eradicated. Guyau quotes Mark Pattison's report of a visit to a Comtist service in London. He described it as three persons and no God.

Guyau accordingly proceeds quite serenely to the substitution of Doubt for Faith. In place of accepting ready-made Dogmas we are to be ourselves the creators of our beliefs. What is to be cultivated is the sentiment of the beautiful and love of the fine arts. Faith being the affirmation of the reality of things incapable of objective verification: attributing to the uncertain the same reality as to the certain. Consequently Philosophy is preferable to Religion, since the former distinguishes between degrees of probability. Experience of life, however, compels the author to admit that we are sometimes forced, if we are to act at all, to treat some things which are uncertain as if they were possessed of certainty. But this experience he thinks exceptional. He is of course well aware that Kant thought otherwise. Kant made faith predominate in morals over Reason. Kant therefore is dismissed. There is no categorical imperative, no moral law within before which conscience is constrained to bow. Guyau takes refuge in the paradox that Doubt is itself a form of the religious sentiment. Yet he went some way further when he wrote: "I do not know, I doubt, I hope."

The Future of Religion

So we are brought back as usual to the old dilemma:

> A life of faith diversified by doubt,
> A life of doubt diversified by faith.

Guyau appears unconscious how heavily he has weighted the scales against Faith, as if doubt were identical with disproof. He asserts that with the advance of science the religious sentiment properly so called must disappear. Philosophy indeed will survive, because that is the instinct of speculative inquiry, and is an indestructible sentiment. But these are assertions.

The valuable element in the religious sentiment, and apparently the only permanent element in it, according to the author, seems to be the idea of association. He aspires to a free association of individual thinkers with their various and variable beliefs, all being regarded as hypothetical and inadequate expressions of the truth. There is to be also in the future an association of wills, on the basis of solidarity and the brotherhood of man. Small importance is attached to the objection that it will be difficult to secure popularity for these ideas in the absence of Religion. For the most egotistical must own that it is impossible to live entirely to oneself. Self-interest itself requires restriction of our activity. Guyau has the greatest faith in the sentiment of generosity. Although he thinks that Moralists have said too much of sacrifice, yet the great surrender of life, courage in face of death, is not peculiar to

Religious Thought in France

Religion. But he will not allow that the thought of what lies beyond Death need be brought in.

There is also to be an association of an aesthetic character, the cult of the fine arts and of Nature. And the more the dogmatic religions are wakened the greater the need that art should be strengthened. Beside every public library there must be gardens, where in fine weather one may read and write in the open air.

In the future then the great metaphysical ideas are to replace the dogmas of the Faith. The author has advanced from asserting their doubtfulness to assuming their unreality.

These reflections and speculations on the prospect of a future in which there is no Religion may be supplemented by a remarkable Essay written some years later by Delvolvé, on "Rationalism and Tradition," in the *Bibliothèque de Philosophie Contemporaine*. The problem discussed in Delvolvé's Essay is—How to make Lay Morality effective without the assistance of Religion.

Accordingly, he explains what instruction should, in his opinion, be given to young men and young women in order to train them for social life. They were to be taught principles of conduct without any idea of God. He had a firm belief in secular Morality, but none whatever in Religion. He observed that young men and women were being instructed in places of higher education that marriage, which is the primary

The Future of Religion

form of social life, must be founded on the free mutual consent of the sexes, and that the obligations which arise out of that free contract should be based on the fundamental principles of the dignity of human beings. On this instruction Delvolvé's reflection is that he does not doubt the value of this idea, nor its influence on the philosophically disposed; but he fears that to the minds of average young men and women it will seem empty and prove without effect.

Delvolvé's reason for misgivings about the persuasiveness of Morality without Religion is that the facts of history obliged him to own that moral ideas, however stable we may wish them to be, are only relatively permanent. They are subject to change. Where Religion does not exist the Christian belief in the finality of Moral decisions disappears. And it does not require much alteration in a man's circumstances to induce him to adopt anti-patriotism instead of patriotism, and polygamy instead of monogamy. He may find fairly strong incentives within himself to both. The more independent the modern man may feel, the more inclined he is to adopt what conduct he prefers. He has a profound belief in progress, in the superiority of the present to the past, and he repudiates any notion of being guided by the experience and traditions of the ages. He is impatient of restraint. And any idea which imposes restrictions on his freedom is met at once with an inclination to resist.

Delvolvé saw quite plainly that the younger generation in France at the end of the nineteenth century was by no means disposed to accept the idea of family life as it was in the past, nor to take it for granted that the family is the completed stage of human progress. It is exactly what they were not prepared to admit. What was actually progressing was unmistakably a relaxing of the family relationships, and of the marriage bond in particular. The conspicuous disintegration of family life, which is a marked characteristic of our time, does not encourage the rising generation's respect for the Traditions of sexual relationship, which have for many centuries prevailed.

Delvolvé is not at all convinced that it is very effective to lay stress on the happiness which married life confers. Sincerity compels him to add that in reality married life demands perpetual sacrifice. Without continual mutual effort harmony can never be sustained. It requires self-renunciation for the sake of the children. It involves suffering in proportion to sensitiveness and to tenderness; the enduring of abiding cares, and the possibilities of being requited by sorrows, bitter disappointments, and cruel ingratitude.

Conditions like these must in all sincerity be set before young men and women. They may have seen something of it in the lives of their parents. To speak exclusively of Happiness is to leave them in deception.

Accordingly this advocate of secular Morality feels misgivings whether the ideas which he is able to impart are adequate to meet the strain which will be encoun-

The Future of Religion

tered, and whether they are strong enough to fortify the man and the woman for the burdens they will inevitably have to bear.

He is a thoughtful person this secular moralist. He sees that the moral troubles of married life arise from weakness of the will, or from failure in the man or in his wife to be conscious of the reality of their union. Weariness of each other's company, mutual failure to understand, impatience, and restlessness, these are, he feels, among the ordinary causes of mutual unhappiness. Harmony is very difficult to attain. Modern marriage seems too often haunted by a miserable yearning after its dissolution. Separation is suggested as a remedy for feebleness of will and instability of character. And the suggestion does not conduce to increase their unity.

This advocate of secular Morals acknowledges his admiration for the Christian doctrine of self-restraint. The ideal realized in the person of Jesus, the characters of the Virgin Mother and of the Saints, renders them to the Christian objects of imitation invested with Divine authority, objects of love which calls forth what is noblest in human nature. To the Christian, Marriage is a Sacrament; that is to say, a Divine enactment accomplished by the mediation of the Religious Society of the Church. This Divinization of the moral ideal has created an heroic exaltation of love, which is the only effective safeguard against the brutality of the senses.

Religious Thought in France

There is in these remarkable sentiments much that recalls the words of Lecky in his *History of European Morals*, where he says that it is the peculiarity of the Christian types of character that while they have fascinated the imagination they have also purified the heart. "The tender, winning, and almost feminine beauty of the Christian Founder, the Virgin Mother, the agonies of Gethsemane or of Calvary, the many scenes of compassion and suffering that fill the sacred writings, are the pictures which for eighteen hundred years have governed the imaginations of the rudest and most ignorant of mankind. . . . More than any spoken eloquence, more than any dogmatic teaching, they transform and subdue his character, till he learns to realize the sanctity of weakness and suffering, the supreme majesty of compassion and gentleness."

Lecky did not hesitate to add that "there can be little doubt that the Catholic reverence for the Virgin has done much to elevate and purify the ideal of woman and to soften the manners of men."

The Englishman and the Frenchman, both outside the Christian Faith, acknowledge in very memorable terms the practical power that Religion can exert and has exerted. They both appreciate the effectiveness of the ideas which Religious belief involves. They recognize that, when it is genuinely embraced, it strengthens human weakness and instability in a very memorable degree. Yet neither of the two men believe that Religion corresponds with reality.

The Future of Religion

And here we reach the most singular feature of Delvolvé's book. He fully admits that the absence of religious inspiration is a serious defect in the programme and the resources of the secular Moralist. He looks about to discover a substitute for the idea of God. He wants to find some non-religious idea capable of exerting the same effect on emotion and will which religious ideas have formerly produced. He thinks his search has been successful. He recommends that in the place of Deity we should substitute Nature. In praise of Nature he grows lyrical. There is a unity of being between Nature and Man. There is a real communion between them. Both are working towards one end. He rises to assurance of universal optimism and faith in the certain victory of his aspirations.

To enlarge on the insecurity of the basis on which this structure is built would be superfluous. One reflection, however, is difficult to resist. The writer acknowledges that Religion gives incentives and ideals and inspirations to conduct which Morality without Religion is unable to provide. Consequently what is in his opinion an illusion is more effective to moral elevation than what in his opinion is the Truth. Of course if the Universe contained no Deity we should have to make the best we could of the impersonal Nature, which is all that would be left. But Delvolvé could not induce himself to think that irresponsible force is equivalent to a personal God, and that life would not be made immeasurably poorer by the exchange.

CHAPTER X

The Influence of Bergson

TWENTY-FIVE years have elapsed since Bergson produced his arresting book, *L'Evolution Créatrice*. His analysis of the limitation of intelligence and its capacity within the sphere of the material and the practical rather than in that of the ultimate problem of existence—is unforgettable. So also is his criticism on Herbert Spencer. Bergson is of Jewish ancestry. His matured reflections are now published to the world in *Les Deux Sources de la Morale et de la Religion*. The reception which this book has met is striking. Three separate volumes have been written about it in French. One of the three by Alfred Loisy—critical and negative, much as we should expect. Another is *Le Dieu de Bergson, par Emile Rideau*, sympathetic and appreciative, written from the Catholic standpoint. Even yet more full of admiration is the opinion expressed in the *Dublin Review* for January of 1934, that Bergson's last work "is the most magnificent apology of Christian mysticism ever published by a philosopher, foreign to Christianity by his origins."

Certainly the work is a severe criticism of Intellectualism. Continuing his estimate of the intellect as adapted to material things rather than spiritual, Bergson interprets Religion in the following way.

The Influence of Bergson

Religion is first a defensive reaction of Nature against the dissolving influence of the intellect.

Illustrating this principle in the distinction between the animal and the man, Bergson points out that the animal does not know that it must die. That knowledge would serve no useful purpose. For its purpose is that it should live. Man, however, knows that he must die. Nature in endowing him with intelligence has produced this knowledge. But nature opposes to the idea of the inevitableness of death the idea of the continuance of life after death. Accordingly we reach a second characteristic of religion. Religion is the defensive reaction of Nature against the representation made by the intellect, of the inevitableness of Death.

Proceeding in this study of the psychological facts in man, Bergson confronts the fact that Religion is co-extensive with the human race, and appears to belong to our Nature. Nature indeed assigns a definite function to religion. Whereas man is by nature essentially social his intelligence leads him to reflect that it is often to his individual advantage to neglect the interests of the social order. Here then we reach a third characteristic of Religion. It is the defensive reaction of Nature against such exercise of the intellect as may be injurious to the individual and destructive to social order.

After these reflections on the characteristics of Religion in general, and the function which it appears to fulfil in the life of man, Bergson proceeds to consider religious individuals, outstanding examples of religious experience. Here he deals with critical difficulties and objections against the reality of Religion. In the first place, how can we rest assured that the religious experience of these individuals is as real as scientific experience is. This religious experience is exceptional, and it cannot be verified as a scientific experience can. Bergson replies: To make these two cases parallel would require that the scientific experiment is always susceptible to repetition. He illustrates the time when Central Africa was an unknown land. What the geographers did was to rely on the report of an explorer provided that they were sufficiently guaranteed of his sincerity and his capability. Livingstone's travels were for a long time inscribed upon our maps. If the criticism is raised that verification was possible in theory if not in fact, and that other travellers were free to investigate, and that the indications on the map were only provisional and awaited final verification, Bergson replies that he agrees. But the experiences of the explorer in religion can also be verified in theory if not in fact. And those who are capable of investigation are at least as numerous as those who had the energy and courage of Stanley who discovered Livingstone. But more than that. Beside those outstanding personalities who advance to the end of the mystic way of Religion, there are many people who advance at least some part of the way. And here Bergson refers to the case of William James, who declared that he

The Influence of Bergson

had never experienced these religious states. But Bergson notes that William James added the impressive remark that when he heard a religious man relate his experience it awakened an echo within himself.

But granted that there are persons to whom Religion is an unknown experience. Are there not persons for whom music is only a noise; persons who grow indignant and are personally aggrieved when they encounter musicians? Would the existence of individuals who have no ear for music justify the inference that there is no reality in the musician's experience? Is it not reasonable to apply this analogy to Religion? Mystical experience creates a presumption in favour of its validity.

Bergson claims that in this analysis he is following the facts of Theology which led to the conception of an *élan vital* and an *évolution créatrice*. He is not constructing metaphysical speculations, but summarizing the facts of Nature.

The Universe does not consist merely of matter. Two realities are given in Nature—matter and life. The vital current and brute matter are the two complementary aspects of creation. The vital current which traverses matter and is no doubt the reason why matter exists, is simply a fact in Nature. A further fact confronting us is that beings have been called into existence who are destined to love and to be loved. Creative energy manifests itself as love. Here the men of experience in Religion declare that the object of this love is God. They testify that God has need of us as we have need of God. Thus Creation is represented as an enterprise of God to create responsive beings and to make them capable of His love.

There is a further objection which Bergson answers. These men of religious experience are men of visions and of dreams. How can we trust visionary and imaginative people? The answer given is that, while it is quite true that religious experience included visions and dreams, it is also true that the experiencers drew a clear distinction between their dreams and their communion with God. They attach small importance to the former. They concentrate upon the latter as essential.

Bergson insists that when the interior state of the men of outstanding experience in religion is studied it is strange that anyone should regard them as mental invalids. Average people live in a state of unstable equilibrium. Healthiness of mind is as difficult to describe as healthiness of body. But there is a substantial intellectual healthiness which is rare but unmistakable. Such health of mind displays itself in practical capacity, in the power to adapt oneself to circumstance, in firmness blended with dexterity, in a shrewd ability to discriminate between what is possible and what is not, in a directness which triumphs over obstacles, and in superior good sense. Now these characteristics are exactly what the mystics manifest. That is to say that whenever the average human being

The Influence of Bergson

lives in a state of unstable equilibrium, these outstanding personalities under the influence of Religion seem to harmonize their faculties and unify their whole being. S. Paul and S. Catherine of Sienna are suggested as examples.

The moral of Bergson's work is plain. Religion deserves far more serious and deliberate attention than it receives from the generality of men. It shows the unreasonableness of indifference. And it shows this by an appeal to the facts of Nature. It prepares the way to impartial consideration, and is arresting marked attention not only in the country where it was written.

Bergson has acquired remarkable influence in France. He has won the support of a number of thinkers. Fonsegrive, in the *Annales de Philosophie Chrétienne* (1911, pp. 225–244), agrees with the theory of Intuition, and connects it with the estimate of values. But nothing could be more enthusiastic than the importance attached to Bergson's philosophy by Edouard le Roy, who devotes an entire volume to its exposition, opening with the following rapturous expressions:

"There is a thinker whose name is to-day on everybody's lips, who is deemed by acknowledged philosophers worthy of comparison with the greatest, and who, with his pen as well as his brain, has overleapt all technical obstacles, and won himself a reading both outside and inside the schools. Beyond any doubt, and by common consent, M. Henri Bergson's work will appear to future eyes among the most characteristic, fertile, and glorious of our era. It marks a never-to-be-forgotten date in history; it opens up a phase of metaphysical thought; it lays down a principle of development the limits of which are indeterminable; and it is after cool consideration, with full consciousness of the exact value of words, that we are able to pronounce the revolution which it effects equal in importance to that effected by Kant, or even of Socrates."*

* Edouard le Roy, *A New Philosophy*, English trans. 1913, pp. 1, 2.

CHAPTER XI

Biblical and Historical Studies among Catholics in France

CATHOLIC writers seem agreed that Biblical Studies were in a very feeble condition in France about the middle of the nineteenth century. Indeed, as late as 1875 it was by no means what it should have been. Few Scriptural Commentaries were being written. Bellamy, himself a Catholic historian of the period, refers to a few insignificant instances, and concludes: "Voilà tout ce qui représentait l'exégèse catholique en France."* The principal figure in Biblical inquiry was Vigouroux (died 1905), for many years representative of these studies, a critic of ultra-conservative type. His *Manuel biblique* in four volumes ran through many editions (1879, etc.).

It was only towards the close of the nineteenth century that Authority at Rome intervened on the newer Biblical criticism. It seems that the Article by Mgr. d'Hulst, Rector of the Catholic Institute in Paris, contributed to the *Correspondant*, in 1893, on the Question biblique, arrested the attention of Leo XIII. d'Hulst, who mediated between the older and the newer schools of Biblical study, was suspected of being

* Bellamy, p. 47; cf. also Grandmaison in Baudrillart, *La Vie Catholique*, pp. 264–265.

under the influence of Loisy, at that time on the Staff of the Institute. The Rector was summoned to Rome, had interviews with the Pope, and explained the motives which led him to write his Article. The Pope appreciated the reasons, but was not satisfied. He held that authors might be spared, but errors must be condemned. That was on the Augustinian maxim, *diligite homines interficite errores*. This attitude the aged Pope maintained until his death. It would be a mistake to attribute to Leo XIII liberal opinions. He never held them. On this fact historians seem agreed.* Leo is said to have regarded the matter rather from the political standpoint of expediency. His Encyclical of 1893† asserted the value of Biblical Studies, but directed prudence and submission to the traditional teaching.

On the Catholic side Bellamy says that theology has undoubtedly gained by Biblical criticism, since it has been compelled thereby to verify the validity of Biblical texts on which its arguments were based, and thus to place its proofs on a more sure foundation. Yet at first sight its losses appear to have exceeded its gains. As an example he refers to the passage on the Three Heavenly Witnesses in 1 S. John v. 7, which previously served as a proof of the Catholic doctrine of the Trinity. There were protracted and vigorous discussions about this text "even among learned Catholics." And the Congregation of the Inquisition felt obliged to intervene in favour of the disputed

* cf. Maurice Pernot, pp. 221–222.   † *Providentissimus*.

passage in 1897. Their declaration was that one could not with security deny or doubt its authenticity. But nevertheless, says Bellamy, the precise purport of this decision has itself been the subject of delicate discussion, and has not prevented several conservative-minded theologians, such as the Benedictine Janssens, from setting aside in Trinitarian Theology this verse about the three heavenly witnesses. It appears to be now proved, adds Bellamy, that this verse was not contained in the Latin text up to the ninth century. Was it originally in the Vulgate? It is permissible to doubt.*

The Pontifical Institute of Biblical Studies was officially decreed by Pius X in 1909. The principal influence was entrusted to the Jesuits. Both the Benedictine and Dominican Orders included biblical scholars of acknowledged reputation. The Dominican School of Jerusalem, under the leadership of Lagrange, was already contributing effectively to the advance of Biblical Studies. Lagrange, himself an accomplished scholar, combined remarkable appreciation of modern critical methods with cautious regard for Authority, and firm adherence to the unchanging Dogmas of the Faith. Neither Benedictines nor Dominicans, however, were permitted to exercise influence in the Pontifical Institute. An historian† says that the Dominicans were

* See further *Vacant, Etudes théologiques sur le Concile du Vatican*, i, p. 405.
† Maurice Pernot, *Politique de Pius X*, pp. 228–229.

Religious Thought in France

considered too liberal, and the publications of Fr. Lagrange were tolerated, but their spirit was not approved.

In the opinion of an independent critic from without,* the Biblical Commission was incapacitated by its very constitution. Placed under Jesuit control, it naturally produced only what Pius X expected of it. It was composed, says Guignebert, without any regard to the proper qualifications of its members. It has distinguished itself by decisions which have naturally distressed the more instructed friends of the Church. It may produce professors of a certain pious type, but it fills independent and learned men with deep resentment. At the same time Guignebert owns that valuable studies in history and exegesis can emerge from the Biblical Institute. But the *Acta Apostolicae Sedis* of January 5, 1921, declares that inerrancy extends to every part of the Bible, and that every assertion of a sacred writer is exempt from mistake.

In 1890 the learned French Dominican Lagrange began the splendid series of New Testament Commentaries which have made his name of world-wide reputation. It has, however, been questioned whether his great volumes exert much influence over the ordinary Parish Priests in France.

Lagrange himself came under the adverse criticism of Rome and received a warning, published officially

* Guignebert.

Biblical and Historical Studies among Catholics in France

in the *Acta Apostolicae Sedis* of June 29, 1923, that his Biblical commentaries were not to be allowed in Seminaries until they had been corrected. Lagrange wrote from Jerusalem expressing his distress and his submission, and no decision consigning his works to the *Index* was published. But he had received a warning which could not fail to have effect in imposing a caution and restraint, rendering the work of a Biblical expositor embarrassing and more difficult. Readers of his commentaries have felt that they are in places affected by the apprehension of disapproval from authorities in the Roman Congregations.

Very memorable was the interest displayed by the French Church in Patristic Studies during the nineteenth century. The splendid re-issue of the Benedictine edition of the Fathers by Gaume, and Abbé Migne's Latin and Greek Patrology, are an astonishing achievement—invaluable for their extensive range, rendering the writings of the early and mediaeval theologians accessible to students as they had never been before. This monumental reproduction of primitive Christian literature is in itself a very significant indication of Catholic desire to maintain identity with the Christian centuries. It eclipses altogether in its massiveness and extent the Library of the Fathers which a similar desire produced at the beginning of the Oxford Movement.

Duchesne's *History of the Church* was consigned to the *Index* in Rome in 1912. A Catholic theologian,

Religious Thought in France

Léonce de Grandmaison* accounts for this condemnation on the ground of the author's incessantly ironical tone, and of his omission of developments in his exposition of facts and doctrines which the Catholic instinct imperatively required.

Toward the close of the century a very valuable series of works on the history of the Church and Doctrine was produced by a remarkable group of French priests, including Mgr. Baudrillart, Tixeront, Allard, Dom Cabrol, Dom Leclercq. Scholars of the very first rank, they have laid the student world under great obligations. Tixeront's three volumes of *History of Dogma* are outstanding for their brilliant clearness and mastery over a wide and complicated sphere. Allard is indispensable for the *History of the Persecutions*. Dom Cabrol for his liturgical learning, and Dom Leclercq above all for his immense edition in French of Hefele's *Councils of the Church*.

The career of the Abbé Henri Brémond is of exceptional interest to Englishmen, owing to his connection with our country, and to his monumental and extensive work on the religious spirit in France. He is not easily separable from the Modernist Movement with which he was intimately associated. He was on the friendliest terms with Loisy, von Hügel, and the principal writers of that School both in England and in France. His greatest intimacy of all was with Fr. Tyrrell. To von Hügel he was the embodiment of

* In Baudrillart, *La Vie Catholique*, p. 287.

Biblical and Historical Studies among Catholics in France

youthful freshness, frank and sympathetic nature, and intellectual ability. Like Tyrrell, Brémond was for years a Jesuit. He resided in England over a considerable period, taking the keenest interest in the Oxford Movement and in English religious life. He published his impressions for the enlightenment of his own nation in a volume called *L'Inquiétude religieuse.* It consists of a series of sketches of Newman, of Pusey, of Ideal Ward, together with reviews of Purcell's *Life of Manning*, which he regarded as a monument of indiscretion, and of Mrs. Wilfred Ward's novel, *One Poor Scruple*, which he subjected to sympathetic criticism. von Hügel judged that Brémond appreciated more than any Frenchman of his acquaintance the English religious spirit, and that he greatly revered the supernatural graces which he found among Anglicans.

Newman above all other Englishmen attracted Brémond. The Jesuit devoted a careful study to the *Essay on Development.* He asserted boldly that "Catholic Theology had shown its providential vitality in accepting, after some hesitation, the doctrine of Newman." It may be questioned whether this assertion was not a little premature.

Brémond, after years' experience withdrew from the Jesuits, in a quite canonical way, and with the authorization of his General, from an atmosphere which to a person of his Liberal associations was not likely to remain congenial, although it is said that in departing he retained the friendships that he had formed among them. From that time he held the position of a secular priest.

Brémond is chiefly remembered by Englishmen for the part which he took at the funeral of Fr. Tyrrell. The story has been told by Miss Petre in her life of Tyrrell, and by Loisy in the third volume of his Memoirs. Tyrrell was dying. He was still under excommunication. During the last days he was not in a state to sign any retraction. When he was buried in the Anglican cemetery at Storrington, the Abbé Brémond briefly explained that nothing was being done that could suggest a schismatic or sectarian attitude, and then repeated some prayers beside the grave. For this act, which Loisy characterized as courageous and humane, Brémond was suspended from ecclesiastical functions.

The Abbé took refuge in religious literature. His next venture was a life of S. Chantal. In the Roman *Index of Prohibited Books* Brémond's volume was condemned. That was in 1913. The author submitted. What precisely was the reason for this condemnation is not clear. Loisy calls the book a jewel of Christian and literary perfection. Miss Sanders, in her life of the same saint, describes Brémond's work as a brilliant monograph withdrawn from circulation.

In 1926 Brémond was elected to the French Academy in succession to Duchesne. It was no easy task for a priest in France to characterize the qualities of his eminent predecessor, whose work, like his own, was on the *Index*, in terms that were likely to satisfy Official Catholicism either in France or in Italy. Loisy gives it as his opinion that Brémond's speech was a model of panegyrical discretion. But the result was secured by evading critical problems and confining attention to psychology.

Brémond published in 1929 another work bearing the enigmatic title of *L'Abbé Tempête*. It was a life of de Rancé, reformer of the Monastery of La Trappe. The book is an extraordinary production: brilliant, but satirical in the extreme, displaying the reformer's inconsistencies and infirmities in a perfectly pitiless light. There is no wonder that a Cistercian Monk, amazed and indignant over these pages, felt constrained in defence of his founder to draw another and a very different picture of de Rancé's Life and Character. In 1931 there appeared *The Real de Rancé, illustrious penitent and Reformer of Notre Dame de la Trappe*, by Ailbe Luddy, of the Cistercian Order, published by the firm of Longmans. "M. Henri Brémond, of the French Academy," says the writer, "is a man of much literary taste and wide culture, with a special gift for satire." Luddy declared that the book "presented to the reader as an authentic portrait of a saintly monk was really a caricature. *The Abbé Tempête* might answer very well as a psychological novel, it is admittedly a clever piece of writing, but as a biography of the Reformer of La Trappe it can only be characterized as a travesty of truth."

Religious Thought in France

Our sympathies are with the Cistercians. Brémond was not the man to write about de Rancé. And this satirical work is strange. During the last seventeen years of his life Brémond was devoting himself to absorbing study of French devotional writings, which appeared in his monumental work, *Histoire Littéraire de Sentiment Religieux en France*. This analysis of religious psychology is traced from the time of S. François de Sales down to Pascal, and with an anticipation of Fénelon. Eleven huge volumes are before us, and yet the labourer's undertaking is left unfinished. It is of course on this wonderful work that Brémond's reputation rests. The sustained interest, the tireless energy, the keen but sympathetic criticism render the whole a very memorable achievement. The earlier portion has been already introduced to English readers by S.P.C.K. With that Society remains the enterprise of making Brémond as well known in England as he is in France.

CHAPTER XII

Catholic Studies of Dogma in France

IT is only possible to select in the present chapter a few outstanding Catholic theologians in France, and only a few special subjects of their study. In the second half of the nineteenth century many important dogmatic works were issued on the Catholic side. Of these the following are here selected. On the Deity of Jesus Christ, Lebreton, and Léonce de Grandmaison. On the doctrine of Redemption, Rivière. On the Holy Trinity, the four volumes of the Jesuit de Régnon. On the Eucharist and on the Church, Batiffol.

Attention has been deliberately confined to the doctrines in which the Newer Protestantism departed from the Historic Faith, and which by contrast Catholicism upheld. The struggle between Gallicanism and Ultramontanism which culminated at the Vatican in 1870 is fully treated in many other places, and is not reconsidered here.

The theory of Development in Theology suggested in Möhler's *Symbolism* was translated from German into French in 1876.

The contents of Möhler's memorable book were further popularized in France by Georges Guyau, who published a very full analysis of the work, together with a most appreciative outline of its author's life. The

Religious Thought in France

influence of Möhler's celebrated work in France has been considerable. Witness the elaborate volume by Vermeil. The account which Vermeil gives of Möhler's exposition of the value of the Church is a remarkable tribute to the German theologian's exposition of the Catholic idea. The Church is the concrete manifestation of Christ. Catholics do not regard the Redeemer as a person who lived eighteen centuries ago and then disappeared. He is not a person about whom they possess only some historical reminiscences. Christ lives perpetually within the Church. This perpetual presence is concentrated in the Eucharistic Sacrifice. Our Lord Himself in what is enacted at the altars of the Church is actually there. He is there in His characteristic quality of Redeemer and Reconciler. He is continuing that function in the midst of sinful humanity. The Eucharist is not a mere reminder of historic facts growing ever more and more remoter in the past. It is a perpetuation of Redemptive sacrificial realities in the living present. The Christ of the Crucifixion and the Christ of the Eucharist are the same Eternal Son of God. In the Eucharist Christ still offers Himself to the Father for the sins of the world. The Eucharist is still part of Christ's Redemptive work. The Death on the Cross does not save any man until it is brought home to the man and he becomes identified with it. And this application and appropriation of the Redemption is secured in the Eucharist. The Cross removes

Catholic Studies of Dogma in France

the obstacles to reconciliation between God and man. The Eucharistic Sacrifice brings that reconciliation to the individual soul.

Men are not worthy by themselves to offer themselves to God. The assembled congregation confesses its sins, and longs to appropriate the blessings of Christ. The Saviour invisibly present intercedes for them and offers Himself in Sacrifice before the Father. He is the invisible high priest. Thus the Atonement is vividly accomplished in the souls of each generation. The Eucharist Sacrifice is the heart of the process by which the souls of men are actually redeemed.

Is not devotion of this kind Christian and living? Is not God therein adored in spirit and in truth? Certainly it depends on belief in the reality of the Incarnation. If God has been made Man, then the Eucharistic Sacrifice illustrates the perfection of humility. It is extraordinarily realistic, based on the invisible presence and activity of the objective historic Christ.

Thus the Eucharistic sacrifice in no way detracts from the Sacrifice upon the Cross. The one presupposes the other, and perpetuates it. The Sacrifice in the Eucharist saves no man by its own action apart from the worshipper's co-operation. Neither does the Sacrifice of the Cross.

The History of Christendom shows, with regard to Creed and Sacraments and Ministry, the development of a religious organism into fuller self-consciousness and completeness. Christ lived and preached a new

Religious Thought in France

Religion. Round Him His disciples were grouped. Among them He chose the few who were to become the solid centre of the primitive Church, and by the power of His Spirit would continue His work. Christ made the Apostles the means of securing unity.

I

A scholarly critical exposition of the Origin of the Dogma of the Holy Trinity is that by Fr. Lebreton,* Professor at the Catholic Institute of Paris. While replying to German criticism the French writer makes considerable use of English scholars, such as Sanday and Swete. The general character of his treatment of the subject may be illustrated from the following. He lays stress on the significance of the method adopted by our Lord in Teaching. Christ elicits rather than dictates, endeavouring to awaken thought progressively in His hearers by word and act, rather than utter declarations which for them would be premature. An instance of this method is the question, "Whom do men say that I am." Another is the statement, "I have many things to say unto you, but ye cannot bear them now."

Lebreton also lays stress on the fact that our Lord never identifies the Sonship of His disciples to the Father with His own. While He teaches them to say

* Second edition, 1910.

Catholic Studies of Dogma in France

Our Father, He Himself never speaks in that way. He says,* "Your Father" and He says, "My Father." He says: "I appoint unto you a Kingdom, even as My Father hath appointed unto Me." "I send forth the promise of My Father upon you." "Your Father which is in Heaven." "Your heavenly Father knoweth that ye have need of all these things." This distinction, says Lebreton, is habitual and can only have been imperiously required by our Lord's consciousness of the difference between a Sonship which was theirs, and the Sonship which was His. All this is brought out even more definitely in S. Matthew xi. 25-27 and S. Luke x. 21-22, where the Father and the Son are represented in perfect mutual comprehension. Lebreton reflects that in all the history of the Dogma of the Trinity we do not find a revelation of the Son of God more intimate and more exalted. Of all the Trinitarian texts in the New Testament the Baptismal Formula is, in Lebreton's view, the most explicit. Ménégoz's objection that if the disciples of Jesus had regarded their Master as an Incarnation of Jehovah they would have offered sacrifice to Him, is answered with the reflection that if it had any value it would prove that the Church did not believe in Christ's Divinity, since it offers in the Eucharist the Sacrifice to the Father, but not to the Son. The Teaching of Jesus, reported by the Synoptic Gospels, represents

* S. Luke xxii. 29; S. Luke xxiv. 49; S. Matt. vii. 11; S. Matt. vi. 32.

Religious Thought in France

all the relation of men with God as dependent essentially on their relation with Christ. Lebreton draws out very forcibly that when S. Paul regards the fact that God spared not His own Son as being the supreme demonstration of the love of God for man, the whole value of the Apostle's argument depends on the relation of Sonship in which Christ stands to the Father. What is implied is that the relation between the Son and the Father is different in kind and entirely superior to that of any other in human form.

There are many other important reflections and criticisms in Lebreton's book. These may suffice to illustrate its general character.

II

One of the most important recent productions in French Catholic Theology is the fine work of Léonce de Grandmaison, the Jesuit, on *Jesus Christ, His Person, His Message, His Credentials*, in three great volumes, translated into English in 1934. It is written with a profound knowledge of Protestant and Rationalist criticism, and with a most impressive mastery of modern thought. It stands without a rival for sober judgment, freedom from speculative guesses, and presence of a deeply religious spirit. The third volume is in effect a masterly treatise on the evidences of the Resurrection of Christ and its significance in Religion.

Catholic Studies of Dogma in France

III

Rivière, Professor at the Theological Seminary of Albi, published his important Essay in two volumes on the Doctrine of the Atonement in 1906. It is a careful historical study of the Patristic and Scholastic writers. Rivière was well read in modern German criticism. He condemned the deplorable language in which Bossuet represented a vengeful Deity "hurling all His thunderbolts against His Son." Such conceptions were completely false. Rivière has particularly in view the assertion of Auguste Sabatier, that the New Testament does not teach the doctrine of a satisfaction offered to Diety, and that God had no need to be reconciled with men. Rivière replies to Ritschl's theory, popularized in France by Bertrand, that there can be no question of any Divine anger against sin.

As to our Lord's own Teaching, Rivière says that "Christ never posed as a theologian discoursing on Salvation. . . . He taught the subjective conditions of forgiveness, without prejudice however to the objective conditions which He was to reveal later on." Sabatier "has no right to say that historically there is nothing more certain than that the parables contain all that Jesus understood by His Gospel. We can see Christ's doctrine involves something more. I sanctify Myself means, according to Old Testament ritual, I offer in Sacrifice."

Religious Thought in France

Rivière's conclusion, after a long historical survey, is that theological speculation on the doctrine of the Redemption was not aroused immediately. But the Age of the Fathers was clear that sin has a certain effect on God, the Divine anger at sin is a reality. There is need that God should be reconciled with us. The Fathers therefore saw in Christ's death a sacrifice of Propitiation. Yet their theology of the Atonement is wanting in depth. They frequently furnished the material on which the Middle Ages worked. In the Scholastic period the doctrine was matured. The sacrifice is a godward Satisfaction. There is, Rivière maintains, nothing to cause surprise in the slow unfolding of the doctrine of the Atonement. The more complex a doctrine is the longer it will take to reach its perfect expression.

IV

On the Doctrine of the Holy Trinity there is the massive work of de Régnon, in four extensive volumes. They are called *Studies in Positive Theology*, and trace the historic development of doctrinal exposition right through the Age of the Fathers and the Scholastic period.

As an illustration of the qualities of this most remarkable study of the Dogma on which the entire Christian Religion is based, the Dogma of personal distinctions within the Divine Unity, one instance

Catholic Studies of Dogma in France

may be selected. It is de Régnon's account of the celebrated explanation of the Dogma of the Holy Trinity, given by S. Richard, Prior of the Abbey of S. Victor. S. Richard endeavours to show by an analysis of the nature of Love how profoundly true to reality the Christian Dogma of the Trinity is. The quality of Love is distinguishable into Love of Self and Love of Others. Love of self is natural and essential in every being capable of will. Love is always directed to persons. It cannot strictly be applied to things. S. Gregory says that charity can only exist between two persons at the least. We do not say that a person has charity towards himself. Charity is essentially altruistic. It is disinterested—centrifugal. Friendship is the gift of self to another. The difference between love of self and devotion to another is plain.

Now, argues S. Richard, the plenitude of the Divine perfection cannot be deficient in that which is involved in and constitutes the noblest expression of love. The love of self is natural and comes from God, and has its ultimate reason in God. It must exist in its perfection in God Himself. But also there must be in God the love of Another. Now God is Love. S. Augustine centuries before had given expression to the analysis of Love. There is in love three things—"he that loves, and that which is loved, and love. What then is love, except a certain life which couples, or seeks to couple together some two things, namely, him that loves and that which is loved." That thought, says Augustine, is the starting-point.*

S. Richard recognizes, of course, that the creation is an act of love. But the Creature never can suffice for the capacity of Love which in God is boundless and eternal. Here therefore we penetrate into the Mystery of the Holy Trinity. Love demands the existence in God of a plurality of persons. The theory which Abelard advocated, explaining the Trinity as three qualities in Deity, power and wisdom and love, S. Richard sets aside as hopelessly inadequate, failing entirely to do justice to the nature of Love. Plurality of Persons in Deity is involved in the very nature of perfect Love. But here confronts him the question how far this Plurality is extended. He holds that perfection of love is achieved in the mutual love of two Divine Persons concentrated upon a Third who is their equal in all things, and their equal in Love.

V

Another of the distinguished French theologians of the period was Mgr. Batiffol. The years of his development were passed in the nineteenth, and of his maturity in the twentieth. He was nearly forty when the latter century opened, and from that date he poured into the press volume after volume of doctrinal

* *De Trin*, Book viii. Cap. X, par. 14; cf. Book ix. Cap. II, par. 2.

Catholic Studies of Dogma in France

and historical studies, all of them of considerable importance. He was an outstanding example of the historical School of Theology, the School which rejoiced in the phrase, *théologie positive*. He criticized with friendly severity the philosophical Modernism of Laberthonnière, whose acutely thoughtful essays as Editor of the *Annales de Philosophie Chrétienne*, which was ultimately consigned to the *Index of Prohibited Books*, were far too powerful to be ignored. Laberthonnière, in a review of Rivière's two volumes on the dogma of the Atonement, raised the challenging question whether the idea of a history of dogma was not for a Catholic ambiguous and misleading. Batiffol replied* that the Studies of the Positive School were historical in their method of inquiry, but theological in their aim. They were not speculative theology. Protestantism seemed engaged in a history of dogmas which repudiated dogmatic reality. The history of dogma so understood amounted to the illusions of the Churches. Laberthonnière contended that however full of divine truth dogmatic formulas might be, they were the objects of human elaboration; they had not fallen ready-made from heaven, but were a product of life on earth. Batiffol acknowledged the element of truth which this criticism contained. Undoubtedly ecclesiastical definitions of faith were a matter of human reflection and elaboration. Such phrases as "Of one substance with the Father" did not come from above

* *Questions d'Enseignement Supérieur Ecclesiastique.*

ready-made. The Church arrived at that expression under the guidance of the Holy Spirit. But ecclesiastical definitions are the outcome of original data belonging to the treasures of Revelation. That applies, for example, to the expression, "Son of God." Laberthonnière, as a Catholic, must see that his theory would reduce every Article of the Creed to relativity. Such a definition as "of one substance with the Father" has a static character, is objective and permanent.

Laberthonnière's *Essay on Religious Philosophy* was condemned at Rome in 1906. *The Annals of Philosophy* struggled on for a few more years and came to an end in 1912.

Batiffol, as Rector of the Catholic Institute of Toulouse onward from the closing years of the nineteenth century, exerted great influence over the higher education of younger priests. He was, however, by no means always approved by the Roman Authorities. In January 1911 a Decree of the Congregation of the Index* pronounced condemnation on several works. Among them were Turmel's *Histoire de la Théologie Positive*, and Pierre Batiffol's book, *L'Eucharistie, la Présence réelle et la Transubstantiation*. It was subsequently announced that both authors had submitted. But, of course, the effect on Batiffol's prestige must have been serious. His name was still on the *Index* in 1924. In a later edition of his work he published the following remarks about this experience. "The first

* *Acta Apostolicae Sedis*, 1911, p. 41.

edition appeared in April 1905; the second unaltered edition followed in a hundred days; the third, with detailed corrections, in April 1906, which was exhausted in 1907. The hour was critical." That means that the book was under scrutiny in Rome. And the author adds: "I could not obtain permission from Rome to publish the fourth edition of my book. Fifty numbered copies only were printed, not for sale, but for the use of certain theologians." In 1913 a fifth edition appeared. In the preface the author remarks: "How permission was granted me by competent authority in 1913 . . . the reader will forgive me if I do not here relate, as I consider it would be premature to explain what spontaneous interventions, as effective as distinguished, secured the favourable consideration of Pope Pius X in person, and led to the book being reissued in Rome itself." A peculiar feature of this incident is that Batiffol's third edition appeared with the *imprimatur* of the Archbishop of Toulouse. It was therefore authorized for diocesan use, and yet soon afterwards prohibited from use in any part of the Roman Church.

Of exceptional interest is the series of Batiffol's works about the Church. The first volume of the series is *L'Eglise Naissante et Le Catholicisme*, translated into English under the title, *Primitive Catholicism* (1911). It was designed to correct the Protestant dissociation of the Catholic Church from Christ. The importance of Batiffol's book was fully recognized by Harnack, who wrote a remarkably appreciative criticism upon it. Harnack said that the author had rendered to his Church a most signal service which could not be undertaken with greater special knowledge of the subject. "Well-informed Protestant Historians of the Church will no longer feel scandalized at the statement that some of the principal elements of Catholicism go back to the Apostolic Age and belong to its very heart." Instead of placing a dividing line between the Apostles and Catholicism, Harnack placed it between the Apostles and Christ. The author of the Lectures on the Essence of Christianity could not be expected to do anything else. But Batiffol called attention to the arbitrary suppression of Sayings attributed to Christ, and showed that only by such unconvincing criticism could the division between Christ and the Apostles be maintained.

Batiffol continued to trace in later volumes the History of Catholicism through the time of S. Augustine down to that of S. Leo.

Batiffol is also memorable for his singularly conciliatory and sympathetic attitude towards the English Church. Like the Abbé Portal, and like the great Cardinal of Belgium, Mgr. Batiffol was keenly concerned in the mutual approach of England and Rome. Nothing could be more appropriate than his selection as one of the representatives in the Conversations at Malines. In his pamphlet, *Catholicisme et Papauté*, he discussed the difficulties felt by Anglicans and Russians

Catholic Studies of Dogma in France

on the subject of Papal Authority. His tone is much more generous than that of Duchesne in *Les Eglises séparées*. The difference may be partly accounted for by the fact that Duchesne wrote under other conditions and twenty years before. Batiffol argued with Bishop Gore, and welcomed the fact that the Warden of Keble did not regard leadership on the part of the Papacy as a usurpation. Batiffol's pamphlet, *Catholicisme et Papauté*, was reviewed by the Warden of Keble in *Theology* (October 1926). Dr. Kidd considered that Mgr. Batiffol made some shrewd hits; but that his urbanity was on a par with his skill, and that he wrote for reconciliation and not for victory. Moreover, he made some generous advances. Batiffol held that "the subject of infallibility is not the Pope alone, but the episcopate in union with him." He regretted that Roman theologians have insisted almost one-sidedly on the Pope's infallibility. The Warden of Keble held that the Episcopate and the Pope are related to each other as a College to its head; neither can move without the other. This view of their relation Dr. Kidd says that Mgr. Batiffol accepted.

The comment of the Monks of Union in the journal *Irénikon*[*] was that, since members of the English Church regarded this explanation, which was in reality the commonly held doctrine, as a proof of newly awakened sympathy, the natural inference was that the doctrine had previously too often been asserted in

[*] Vol. i. 1926, p. 310.

Religious Thought in France

a one-sided way, and in a controversial atmosphere which rendered appreciation difficult. The fact, however, remains that discussion about the English Church is now forbidden to the Monks of Union. Mercier and Portal and Batiffol are all departed. Successors animated with a similar spirit are to be desired.

CHAPTER XIII

Preachers in Paris in the Nineteenth Century

THE inauguration of the celebrated Conferences in Paris was due to Mgr. de Quélen, the Archbishop. It is a singular story. de Quélen was a vacillating character, proverbially reluctant to act with any decision. He realized the urgent need, and indeed the craving, for a leader among the younger men. The one outstanding preacher of the time, the object of the young men's desire, was Lacordaire. But then Lacordaire's antecedents were easily turned against him. His association with the former Catholic, now Freethinker, Lamennais, his well-known independence as a politician, his bold uncompromising utterances in the pulpit, naturally alarmed a timid and apprehensive chief. de Quélen's Vicars-general, Dupanloup, and his own successor, Affre, did their best to induce their Chief to act courageously. But the Archbishop expressed his fears that some unguarded utterances of the preacher might lead the Government to interfere. Accordingly de Quélen proposed that the sermons should be written out and submitted to an ecclesiastical authority before they were delivered. The difficulty was that Lacordaire's genius lay in improvisation, and discourses written out before they were delivered would either not represent what he actually said, or else frustrate his special gifts. The Archbishop wavered,* unwilling to be responsible either for keeping Lacordaire in silence or for allowing him to preach. At last, after unconscionable delay, de Quélen gave consent.

The nineteenth century was a century of Orators, memorable in this respect alike in Church and State. Lacordaire was certainly among the chief. It has been truly said that no preacher of that age bore more unmistakably the characteristics of his time than this barrister who became a priest and then a monk. He had a great soul and an ardent imagination, and understood how to speak on the things of eternity in the accents of his age.†

Lacordaire's advantages were immense. Keenly in sympathy with the movements of his time, distinguished for his bold if somewhat theatrical defence of liberty to teach, he held a position in popular opinion, whether friendly or reverse, which was altogether unique. His sacrifice of secular prospects for what to the majority of his age appeared, to say the least, a losing cause, rendered him an object of debate. These distinctions, together with his wonderful gifts of eloquence, of improvisation, of capacity to move and even thrill whole masses of a mixed audience of men, and, above

* Foisset, *Vie de Lacordaire*, 1870, i. 299 ff.
† cf. Brugerette, *Le Prêtre François*, pp. 91, 92. See also De Haussonville, *Lacordaire*.

Preachers in Paris in the Nineteenth Century

all, the depth and intensity of his beautiful devotion to Jesus Christ, gave promise from which great issues might well be expected.

Such was the man who began the Conferences at Paris in Notre Dame in 1837. He looked out over a sea of faces. Foisset says there were six thousand men. Guizot* says that "Lacordaire from the pulpit of Notre Dame, developed, or rather painted, in all their splendour, the truths, the beauties, the moral and social excellences of the Christian Faith and of the Catholic Church." "A numerous auditory, young and old, from the salons and from the schools, believers and freethinkers, flocked round the Abbé Lacordaire, all feeling the attraction, and almost all the charm; many amongst them yielding to the persuasion of that eloquence, so fresh and vivid, and abundant and unlooked for, . . ."

It is impossible to give any adequate idea of the preacher's eloquent improvisations. One famous passage cannot be omitted. It is the splendid appeal to Christ spoken after years of preaching when he came to speak of the Redeemer's Person.

"Lord Jesus, for the ten years that I have spoken of Thy Church to these hearers, it is always essentially of Thee that I have spoken. But to-day I come more directly to thy very self, to that Divine Face which is daily the object of my contemplation; to Thy sacred Feet which I have so often kissed; to Thy loving

* *Meditations*, p. 45.

Hands which have so often blessed me; to Thy Head crowned with glory and with thorns; to that life whose fragrance I have breathed from my birth, which my adolescence misunderstood, and my early manhood recovered, and my maturity adores and proclaims to every creature. O Father, O Master, O Friend, O Jesus, help me more than ever, since being nearer to Thee my hearers must perceive it, that the words of my lips reveal Thy adorable nearness."*

One other passage must be quoted, perhaps the most memorable of all. It is Lacordaire's farewell to Notre Dame.

"Here it was that prostrate upon the pavement of this Temple, I mounted by degrees to the priesthood, and where, after I had long sought for the secret of my vocation, it was revealed to me in this pulpit, which for the last seventeen years you have surrounded with silence and honour. It was here that, returning from a voluntary exile, I brought back the religious habit which half a century of proscription had banished from Paris, and that presenting it to an assembly formidable by its number and diversity, I won your unanimous respect.

"O sacred walls of Notre Dame, sacred vaults that have carried my words to so many intellects deprived of God, altars which have blessed me, I do not leave you; I do but say what you have been to a man, and melt within myself at the remembrance of your bles-

* *Conference* 37, *Year* 1846, p. 7.

sings, like the Children of Israel, who, both at home and in exile, celebrated the memory of Sion.

"And you, gentlemen, generation already numerous, in whom perhaps I have implanted truths and virtues, I am bound to you for the future as I have been in the past; but if one day my strength should be unequal to my will, if you should come to disdain the remains of a voice once dear to you, know that you will never be otherwise than dear, for nothing can in the future prevent you from having been the glory of my life, and from being my crown in eternity."

The rapturous tribute of that most eloquent layman, Montalembert, to Lacordaire as a preacher, is one of the most impressive witnesses to the great Dominican's power.

"No one of us had ever heard the like, and of those who that day heard them, none will ever forget them. They will never forget those days when the chord of the beautiful, the true, the great, and the good, vibrated in their hearts under the might of that voice: those days in which they saw bursting forth from a priestly breast, as from the rock struck by the Divine rod, that impetuous crystal stream, surging and irresistible as an Alpine torrent. Ah! I confidently call around this great and cherished memory all those whom I once saw swelling those serried ranks, quivering with emotion around the pulpit of Notre Dame."*

The Revival of Catholicism advanced by Lacordaire

* Montalembert, *Life of Lacordaire*, p. 148.

Religious Thought in France

was estimated by Guizot, as a statesman and a conscientious Protestant, in terms of remarkable impartiality. He owns that the restoration of Monasticism in Paris placed his political party in a most trying position.

"Great was the general astonishment, and violent were the attacks made upon us, when, with a devotedness to Catholicism even bolder than had been his Conferences at Notre Dame, the Abbé Lacordaire returned from Rome a monk, and a monk of an order which has left more sombre memories behind it than any other, that of S. Dominic."

Yet while expressing no opinion as to the service which monastic orders may render to the Church in the nineteenth century, Guizot reflects in a truly historic spirit that "no well-read man can deny their having, in seasons of chaotic confusion, effectually served the cause, not only of the Christian Faith, but of civilization, of science, and even of liberty."

II

Another of the great preachers at Paris was the Jesuit Ravignan, who occupied the pulpit of Notre Dame in the years 1837–1846. His portrait gives the impression of a very strong personality, firmness of will, austere self-discipline, and serenely invincible faith. He was far more learned and more of a theologian than Lacordaire. His Conferences are rather the products of a studious mind who has found his inspiration in the Scholastic Masters, and is far less intimately acquainted with the actual movements of popular thought. He is deeply devout, incisive, and sententious. But there is nothing of the impetuous torrent or the improvised eloquence of Lacordaire. The training of the one had been in the ordinary world: of the other in the world of religious learning. Ravignan's Conference on the Character of Jesus Christ is widely different from the corresponding interpretation by Lacordaire, lacking the Dominican's beauty and flow of expression, but measured and accurate. Ravignan's Conference on the Eucharist presents a dogmatic sureness and precision which the Dominican preacher would not have equalled. Each had his separate function to fulfil.

Guizot says that Ravignan was surrounded not only by members of his own Church, but by men not remarkable for their faith. He owed this moral authority far less to his talent as an orator than to the thorough sincerity and disinterestedness of his religious character. He was "a stranger to every mental reservation: neither was he a partisan, but solely occupied with the service of God, of his Church, and of his Order, at the same time that he was propagating the faith and enforcing piety." That is a memorable tribute from a Protestant to a Jesuit.*

* Guizot, *Meditations*, 1866, p. 29.

Religious Thought in France

III

During the years 1856 to 1870 the preacher at Notre Dame was the Jesuit Félix.* His conception of the peculiar responsibilities of the pulpit in the Cathedral in Paris is given in his own account. He held that the purpose of the Conferences there was to commend the Christian Religion to the men of the nineteenth century. It was a point of contact between the Christian world and a semi-pagan world living in the very midst of Christendom. It was the function of the preacher in Paris to explain to the masses a religion which they no longer knew. It was a mission quite different from that of the parochial preacher encircled by those who believed already. At Notre Dame the preacher must speak to his contemporaries, in a language which they would understand, truths which they would not attend to hear elsewhere. He must deal with contemporary misconceptions, and the very form of his discourse must reveal its affinities with the spirit of the age.

Acting on this conception of his duty, Fr. Félix chose as his general subject, Progress by Christianity. He knew that Progress was the ideal of his contemporaries. One of the dominant themes of the century appealing strongly to the enthusiasm of the time. So he determined to speak of Progress, understanding, of course, that Progress was Christ. For nearly twenty years Félix carried through that theme.

* *Conférences par*, R. P. Félix, 1856, pp. viii, ix.

Preachers in Paris in the Nineteenth Century

Félix did not possess the genius of Lacordaire, nor were the circumstances of his entrance upon the work as impressive to the popular mind as those of his great predecessor. But he was gifted with remarkable eloquence, a logical and analytical mind, and a considerable intimacy with the spirit of his age.

A contemporary English opinion of Fr. Félix as a preacher is preserved in the Life of Hartpole Lecky. Lecky "went three times to hear Père Félix, who was then said to be the greatest preacher in the world: an extremely eloquent man, perfect rhetoric flowing with unbroken rapidity from the beginning to the end, very sarcastic, admirable action but the substance was not equal to the form."*

Our own great English preacher, Dr. Liddon, says: "I heard Père Félix at Notre Dame. His subject was the Positive Philosophy. His audience almost entirely composed of men—seats being reserved for great literary and political notorieties. His method was wonderfully clear; his style trenchant and incisive; his manner apparently too vehement and passionate for a philosophical discussion. His sarcasm was unsparing, and two or three times the suppressed murmur of applause threatened to become a shout of approbation. He reserved the religious and spiritual touches for his wind-up. They were very effective and beautiful."†

* *Memoir of Lecky by His Wife*, 1909, p. 33.
† *Life of H. P. Liddon*, p. 98.

Religious Thought in France

IV

The next great preacher at Notre Dame was the Carmelite, Père Hyacinthe. He was certainly a born Orator. No one can read his later sermons after his leaving the Roman Church without the impression that he had all the gifts of the popular debater, quick to seize the changeful minds of his audience and to appeal to their emotions. But it is difficult to feel that he was as strong in the devotional adoring relation to our Lord which was conspicuous in Lacordaire.

Hyacinthe's extraordinary power as a preacher soon attracted attention. He was invited to take a course at the Madeleine, where Montalembert heard him and commended him to the Archbishop of Paris, with the result that Darboy appointed him in 1869 to give the Conferences at Notre Dame. Hyacinthe's influence over young men in Paris was immense. Unhappily for him, that very year Pius IX issued his *Syllabus*, in which many modern errors were condemned, and as the progressive generation felt, many mediaeval mistakes were endorsed. It was in a mood of deep discouragement, depression, and misgiving for the future that Hyacinthe came to preach at Notre Dame. His Conference gave grave offence. He was sent for by the General of his Order, and had to go to Rome to explain his utterances. It appears that Pius IX was satisfied with the Preacher's explanation. But Hyacinthe himself was seriously unsettled. He complicated matters

Preachers in Paris in the Nineteenth Century

by imprudent letters to the Press. The fact is that he was more unsettled than his superiors seem to have realized. The Decree of Infallibility was for him a fatal crisis. But it is open to question whether in any case he would have remained in the atmosphere which the dominant school had created. The Preacher of Notre Dame was excommunicated. And it is from any point of view pathetic to reflect that some of his greatest orations were delivered after he had withdrawn from the Catholic Church.

Père Hyacinthe's influence from the pulpit of Notre Dame passed out beyond the limits of France. His utterances arrested attention in England also. It is interesting to remember that Dr. Liddon found it necessary to write warning criticisms against Père Hyacinthe's teaching. "I could only acquiesce in the *a priori* considerations pressed by Père Hyacinthe, on grounds which would incline me to look to Constantinople rather than to Rome for relief." The Supremacy, which Père Hyacinthe at that time advocated, was to Dr. Liddon "an upgrowth of the Western Church, having no real justification in antiquity." It is a singular reflection that, within a year or two of Dr. Liddon's criticism, Père Hyacinthe was teaching on this subject much the same as the great Anglican preacher maintained.*

Certainly one of the most telling orations that Hyacinthe (Loyson) is reported to have made in his

* *Life of H. P. Liddon*, p. 127.

Religious Thought in France

Protestant period is that on the Cross upon the Pantheon.* It was pronounced in 1885. The Pantheon had been appropriated by the State as a burial place of famous people, and ceased to be a Christian Sanctuary. The Cross surmounting the Dome had been pulled down. Loyson pleaded before a very mixed audience that the Cross is always the sign of Christian civilization, the sign of social redemption. He urged that the Pantheon was a National Temple, that a Temple presupposes worship, and that worship implies a doctrine. His speech was frequently interrupted by applause and sometimes by protests. When he came to ask the question—Ought the Cross to be retained on the Dome of the Pantheon—his audience broke into clamours of Yes and No. He asked them whether the Cross had lost in modern France all religious and social meaning? The orator declared, "The Cross, this is my conviction, belongs to the future, and even to eternity. But even if it had no value but to represent the past, it ought still to be respected." Here the speaker's voice was drowned in excited cries of protest and cheering. For some moments it was impossible to continue. Some shouted—The Cross, the Cross; and others—Down with the Cross. Loyson retorted: "You ought not to destroy the Cross. If you have a better emblem, set that above it, an emblem more religious and more social." Voices in the audience proposed a bust of Liberty, the French Flag. Loyson replied: "No

* Loyson, *Ni Cléricaux ni Athées*.

one respects the Flag of our Nation more than I. But it is the emblem of a Nation. The Cross is the emblem of all Nations." That was followed by prolonged applause, in which the orator vainly attempted to make himself heard. When comparative quiet was restored he appealed to his audience as reasonable men. He reminded them that the material Cross was, after all, only a secondary matter. Whatever they might do they could not entirely suppress it. For to do that it would be necessary to pull the Pantheon down altogether. Since the Pantheon is built in the form of a Greek Cross. Expressions of approval and resentment. He acknowledged that the Cross had been profaned, but appealed to them not to leave it to its profaners. Do not forget the tears that it has drawn, nor the devotion which it has inspired. That was met with laughter, to which Loyson replied by quoting Victor Hugo. "You who weep come to the God who has wept." After prolonged pleading, interrupted by violent protests and passionate cheering, the orator ended the conference with the sentence—The Cross is Christianity. It is Civilization. It is Liberty.

v

The next great preacher in the succession at Notre Dame was Monsabré, the Dominican.

Monsabré gave a complete exposition of Catholic Dogma in Paris in a series of Conferences during many years (from 1873 to 1889), distributing his subject into four principal divisions: God, Jesus Christ, Grace and the Sacraments, the Last Things. His Sermons were published in some twenty volumes. The French theologian, Grandmaison, says that they were very widely read in France.*

Monsabré preached in Notre Dame in 1882 a sermon which was substantially a long argumentative defence of the Inquisition. He attributed the horrors to the secular authorities, declared that instruments of torture employed against criminals had been mistakenly attributed to the responsibility of the Church. The sermon was not characterized by impartiality, nor by any acknowledgment of the Church's implication in, or consent to methods of dealing with, unbelief or religious error irreconcilable with the principles of Christianity.

To Hyacinthe (Loyson),† now excommunicated, that sermon was intolerable, and provocative to the last degree. He had himself in former years stood in that selfsame pulpit. And he now gathered all the force of his eloquence in a great oration in reply.

Monsabré is described by one of his hearers as the most authoritative and eloquent preacher of that date, if not the greatest Catholic speaker in France. A graphic account survives of his vigorous appearance, his energetic personality, his forcible style of argu-

---
* In Baudrillart, *La Vie Catholique*, p. 255.
† See *Ni Cléricaux ni Athées*, pp. 139-141.

ment.* Systematic reasonings were set forth with great impressiveness. Exposition of Dogma was his strength. There never was a man who appealed less to imagination. But he filled Notre Dame to overflowing, and his *Conférences*, immediately printed, circulated through France. He compelled Frenchmen to realize that Religion did not consist in vague sentiment, but in very definite Truth.

Monsabré's sermon on the application of Christian principles to social life† is a good example of his preaching and influence in the crowds in Paris. He explained that according to the principles of the Christian Religion there is between all men a fundamental equality of rights and duties; but also in the classification of the members of social life there are providential inequalities, due to irremovable causes. There is between all men an equality in nature, an equality in grace among all those who are Christians, and an equality in destiny. All life ends with the same humiliation in death and corruption, through which, however, God will have all men to be saved. There are also inequalities. Nature shows itself generous to the one and hard and ungenerous to another. The individual inherits in himself the causes which raise or depress him, and create inevitable difference. One is endowed with keen desire to know. Another loses his energies in dreams. One is bold and confident: another uncertain

* Strowski in *La Vie Catholique*, p. 441.
† *Sixth Conference.*

and fearful. Some have strength of will to resist their passions, others are weak of will and easily yield to the dominion of evil instincts. The undeniable fact that men are diversely gifted is no fatal determination of their ultimate qualities and worth. He who has more may sink below him that has less. Everything depends on the use of the gifts of Nature and Grace. But the diversity of gifts does involve social inequalities. The cause of the diversity is the Will of God. The reduction of all diversities to one level of uniformity is not progress, and can only be done by the suppression of talent, of character, of freedom, and results in the deterioration of social life. Social inequalities are not the result of chance or injustice, but of the dispensation of Providence. But they must be modified and perfected by the exercise of Christian love.

Here the preacher drew the painful contrast between Wealth and Poverty. Resources were opportunities of service. The religious maxim was—Honour the Lord with thy substance. Thus Poverty is the personification of the Son of God.

Then Monsabré directed his hearers in fervent impassioned words to the Son of God as Crucified. The Christian must see Christ in the Poor. The Poor man impersonates Jesus Christ. "Inasmuch as ye did it unto the least of these my Brethren, ye did it unto Me." The passionate pursuit of wealth was contrasted with the charity that seeketh not her own. Then followed a powerful appeal to the well-to-do to seek out and befriend the poor. In the old prophetic words, Monsabré called on his hearers to witness that he had set before them life and death, blessing and cursing. He appealed to them by their charity and generous conduct to the less fortunate to choose life, that both they and their seed might live.

That sermon stirred his hearers to the very depths. The emotional French could not restrain their feelings. The audience broke out into loud and fervent applause. The same thing happened years before at the preaching of Lacordaire. Monsabré was disconcerted, and at the time made no remark, but on the following day prefaced his sermon with a dignified appeal that such demonstrations should not be repeated.

VI

The succession of eminent preachers had made the pulpit of Notre Dame a centre of very extensive, almost national interest. Public opinion was keenly concerned about the next occupant. The nomination of a preacher by Cardinal Richard, Archbishop of Paris, was awaited almost with suspense. The story as told by Mgr. Baudrillart, d'Hulst's successor in the Rectorship of the Catholic Institute in Paris, casts an instructive light on contemporary religious feeling among the people. Several among the previous priests to whom the responsibility of rendering the Catholic Religion persuasive to the popular intelligence of

Religious Thought in France

Paris had been pre-eminent for eloquence and power. Their appointment was natural, almost inevitable. In the closing years of the nineteenth century there were several preachers highly gifted, any one of whom might well be chosen. There was, for instance, Didon, the eloquent Dominican, author of admirable sermons against Divorce, and of a highly rhetorical and fervid and picturesque account of the life of Christ. Many people eagerly hoped that Didon would be selected. Opinion was divided. Critics objected. The pulpit of Notre Dame ought not to be the monopoly of the Dominican Order. As a matter of fact it had not been—Jesuits had occupied it as well as Dominicans. When it was announced that the Archbishop had appointed Mgr. d'Hulst, there was a feeling of disappointment. d'Hulst was a thoughtful preacher of very considerable power, unquestionably a theologian, scholastic in his outlook, delighting in the exposition of doctrinal principles, speculative within the sphere of Truth, habituated to reasoning, well aware of the difficulties which Catholicism presented to the modern mind, unhesitatingly acknowledging them, and treating opponents with a sympathy none too prevalent in the ordinary attitude of Catholic authorities in his day. d'Hulst in his earlier days had endangered his own career and the future of the Institution over which he presided by his sympathetic appreciation of liberal tendencies in Biblical criticism. He did his utmost to protect Alfred Loisy and retain him among the lecturers

Preachers in Paris in the Nineteenth Century

at the Institute. But he had been compelled to go to Rome and account for his attitude, and if he escaped a personal censure he learnt the necessity of caution and restraint. Such was the preacher who began the Conferences at Notre Dame in the Lenten Season of 1891, and at intervals continued to be preacher for some six years. Through most of the time he was subject to perpetual adverse criticism from the Press.

An estimate of d'Hulst formed by a contemporary fellow-countryman* is that he combined the interests of a metaphysician with those of a lover of history. This union of the intellectual with the historical is precisely what his age especially needed. His metaphysical interests linked him with the doctrinal past. His love of history and of fact linked him with the special requirements of his time. He deeply sympathized with experimental methods, and felt that Theology must be liberated from *a priori* conceptions. Thus he was adapted to represent Christian Religion to contemporary France.

Baudrillart draws a very instructive contrast between the congregation which Lacordaire addressed, and that which assembled when d'Hulst was preaching. Lacordaire's hearers were of a romantic age, liberal, eager, emotional. For such a congregation Lacordaire's brilliant utterances, bold, impassioned, thrilling, audacious, were marvellously adapted. The hearers of d'Hulst were men trained by scientific education,

* Michelet in *La Vie Catholique*.

accustomed to logical exposition, and adverse to rhetoric. To a congregation of this kind dogmatic and solid instruction, relieved indeed by occasional passages of eloquence which rekindled attention and which sometimes met applause, was best suited.

d'Hulst was a priest of great ability. He did not possess the genius, the popular oratorical power of Lacordaire. He was far more learned, accurate, and precise. His natural bent is suggested by his Conferences previously given at the Catholic Institute, on the scientific value of scholastic philosophy (1886). He was the professor adapting himself to the requirements of popularity. His utterances were by no means spontaneous, but the result of long, laborious preparation. A hearer* compared the sermons at Notre Dame to the Bampton Lectures delivered before the University of Oxford by a fellow of Christ Church who became Canon and Chancellor of S. Paul's Cathedral. Those were the days when a sermon of an hour and three-quarters was not unusual.

VII

Janvier, the Dominican, held the pulpit at Notre Dame from 1903 to 1917.† He delivered an extensive exposition of Catholic Morals, published in some fifteen volumes.

* Baudrillart, *d'Hulst*, ii, p. 489.
† See Grandmaison, in Baudrillart, *La Vie Catholique*, p. 255.

Preachers in Paris in the Nineteenth Century

In the Conferences of Janvier, given in Lent year after year from 1903, and openly commended from the Vatican, the general subject is the Moral Laws of the Church, and again the treatment quite distinct from that of his predecessors. The Conferences are furnished with lists of authorities, with appendices and notes, extending nearly to a hundred pages in a volume of 460. The atmosphere is different. The opponents of the Roman pontiff are denounced. There is a more uncompromising assertion of Authority. Yet there are many forcible passages. The contrast, for example, between the Jewish and the Christian conception of God is drawn out very impressively. God is One, said the preacher. But if He is One He is then alone, and if He is alone how can He be in happiness? If He is not alone how can He be One? He who has united the Angels in fellowship, He who has created social life among men, does He hold Himself aloof from all intercourse? Is He doomed to an appalling solitude? On questions such as these the Old Testament only throws inconclusive gleams. Christ knew what is and what happens in the inner life of the Eternal. He has revealed it and His Authority requires our belief. God is not alone. The Trinity of Persons in a manner which transcends our powers is reconciled with Unity of Nature.

Janvier was held in high esteem by the authorities of the French Church. Beside his Conferences at Notre Dame he was entrusted to be exponent of the Faith on a number of great occasions. At the Consecration of the Jesuit Church of Montmartre in 1919 he preached in the presence of nine Cardinals and nearly a hundred Bishops. He preached again at the Commemoration of Bossuet. It became also his unfortunate distinction to deliver a panegyric on that vitriolic controversialist, Louis Veuillot, whose exaggerations in the Infallibility disputes were too much for the better advocates of that decree.

Janvier knew by his own experience what it was to have thousands of men before him when he preached from the pulpit of Notre Dame. But he also knew that the times in which his lot was cast differed greatly from those in which the Conferences at Paris began. Preaching at Notre Dame in 1913, he recalled to the minds of his hearers the scene when Lacordaire addressed the crowds from that very pulpit some eighty years before. Janvier reminded them that Lacordaire took possession of Notre Dame before an assembly in which all classes, ages, and opinions intermingled. Neither Bossuet nor Bourdaloue had ever won such popularity. Never had Paris been so deeply and widely moved. Such men as Victor Hugo, Lamartine, Chateaubriand, Guizot, Cousin, were all attracted. University professors, magistrates, workmen from the factories, soldiers from the barracks, students from college, literary men and statesmen escaping from the shipwreck of all doctrines, crowded beneath the arches of that Cathedral, and gathered before that Christian

Preachers in Paris in the Nineteenth Century

pulpit which previously they had despised. At first turbulent and derisive, they yielded to one who set them face to face with eternal realities. At times confused, or humbled, or thrilled, they were beside themselves, and twice or thrice in an hour almost involuntarily as if enchanted rose responsively to his words. And so the vast assembly, sometimes persuaded, always deeply moved, bowed itself before the Christ and before His Cross.

Seldom has a great preacher paid a more splendid tribute to a preacher still greater than himself in the very place where his greatest utterances were delivered.* It shows, at any rate, the power of the pulpit in the nineteenth century in France as estimated by those who had the best of reasons to know.

* Janvier, *Fêtes do France*, p. 240.

CHAPTER XIV

The Literary Men attracted to the Church

THE number of literary men in France converted to Catholicism has made a great impression both within that country and beyond it. The approval or actual return to Faith on the part of such writers as Bourget, Coppée, Huysmans, Faguet, and Brunetière, besides Claudel and Péguy is too remarkable to be ignored. Marked attention was directed to these conversions of the literary men in France at the International Congress of Religions in 1913.* It was there attributed to reaction from an idolatrous cult of science and rationalism. Boutroux and Bergson were said to have promoted the same reaction in cultured circles.

Bergson's influence over sceptical thought in France is clearly very considerable. If it were otherwise, a critic would not have written the resentful sentence that Bergson appears to hold in his subtle hands the soul of all the snobs of literature, and produces among them actual and solid conversions. Nor would he find it necessary to say that people were carrying about a work of Emile Boutroux as piously as if it were a missal.† Nor would another critic consider it worthwhile to write a whole volume of somewhat disdainful

* Bernhausen, p. 99.
† Guignebert, p. 253.

The Literary Men attracted to the Church
criticisms on *Les Grands Convertis*, Bourget, Huysmans, Brunetière, and Coppée.

I

It certainly seems true that the attraction of Catholicism to some of the literary leaders in France has been largely, even predominantly, aesthetic or emotional. With the highly strung, artistic, imaginative temperament that is not surprising. It was unquestionably the case with Chateaubriand. His *Génie du Christianisme* is nothing else than an eloquent, even rapturous appreciation of the aesthetic side of religion, its appeal to sentiment. It has been truly said by a fellow-countryman of his own, that Chateaubriand in dealing with Christian verities has only touched upon the surface of things. It may be fairly added that it is difficult to read the *Génie du Christianisme* without the impression that the author was far more concerned with the beautiful than with the true. The outer beauty of Catholicism fascinated him. How far he realized its intellectual splendour he has not made as plain.*

II

The novelist, Huysmans, was deeply moved by the inspiring mystery of the great Cathedral, and by the liturgical solemnity. Receptiveness to the beautiful

* Jules Souben, *L'Esthétique du Dogma Chrétienne*, p. viii, 1898.

in Religion and to the dignity of devotional expression abounds in his eloquent descriptions. The scene has made its powerful appeal to religious sentiment. And of course such appeal to the artistic temperament may open out vistas, definite or vague, into the supernatural realm. It is always possible that in certain literary conversions the great dogmas of Religion had in themselves only a subordinate influence. There are unquestionably cases in which the influence of sentiment is plain, while the influence of dogmatic Truth is obscure or quite uncertain.

III

Bourget, the novelist, in his earlier days had felt like so many of his countrymen the influence of Rationalism as held by Taine. He was thoroughly familiar with the fascination exerted at that time by the Materialist theory that freedom of the will was an illusion which advanced Science had refuted. He was also deeply familiar with the psychology of the passions, and with the practical results on life of sexual irregularities. He was himself gravely immersed in the analysis of animal passion. But in the period of reaction from naturalism, and in his escape from the Rationalism of Taine, he pictured with terrible psychological realism the consequences which immoral relationships and unrestricted indulgence of the lower nature created in social and individual life.

The Literary Men attracted to the Church

In the repulsive, needlessly detailed but fearfully convincing pages of his novel, *Le Disciple*, Bourget displays the practical effect produced on the morals of an intelligent, sensitive, somewhat abnormal pupil by an old Rationalist Professor's negations of the fact that man possessed any freedom of the will, or consequently any moral responsibility. The reader will often wish to open the windows, to let the cold north wind blow through, and force the contaminated atmosphere to escape. But he will be unable to deny the awful truth of the novelist's description of the effects of a false conception of life, and a diseased imagination on character.

As Irving Babbitt finely says, representing Bourget's outlook: "All the nobler aspirations of man, all his notions of conduct, had clustered around the old-time conception of the soul, and of the struggle between a higher and lower self. The weakness of the traditional belief has been followed by such an unsettling of all fixed standards, by such intellectual and moral chaos, that we are inclined to ask whether the modern man has not lost in force of will and character more than an equivalent of what he has gained in scientific knowledge of life."*

An outlook of that kind would obviously dispose towards Conversion.

Bourget maintained that France continues to be a great Catholic country, in spite of government, its

* *The Masters of Modern French Criticism*, p. 239.

Religious Thought in France

electors, its codes, its journals, and in spite of everything.

IV

The attraction of Ferdinand Brunetière to Catholicism has characteristics of its own. He was editor of the *Revue des Deux Mondes*, and member of the French Academy. His tendencies were intellectual, not sentimental. His strength lay in logic, and not in imagination.

Brunetière's whole mind revolted from the absorption in sentiment and passion prevalent in the fiction of his time. In the collection of Critical Essays entitled *Le Roman Naturaliste*, he uttered his protest against that school and its results on popular morality. The detailed analysis of sensuality was not only tiresome, it was sickening. Brunetière quoted the confession of a novelist that he was compelled to learn before he could write on certain subjects, and he could not be completely instructed unless he felt the same emotions in his own experience. The entire absence of philosophic culture distressed him. Brunetière was convinced that each individual is the determiner of his own destiny. That was his outlook on life. Experience proved that there are among us many whose passions are strong and whose wills are weak, who are slaves of their desires rather than masters of their emotions, and that these facts of naturalism cannot be ignored, nor can it be safely taken for granted that men will

The Literary Men attracted to the Church

resist their desires. There are actions which identify us with the animal, and there are actions which separate us from them, and it is by the latter that we are men. No doubt our sensations are part of our nature, but it must be remembered that they are an inferior part. There are actions which are noble, actions which are indifferent, and actions which are distinctly degraded. Consequently the literature which subordinates sensations to thought is the literature which corresponds to reality.

Brunetière's remarkable critical study of the *History of French Literature,* extending over many volumes, brought him into living, sympathetic contact with many of the most famous names of the Catholic past.

In an admirable Essay on Brunetière, Irving Babbitt shows conclusively that the great problem of the French critic's career was to discover a power able to resist the prevalent laxity and self-indulgence of his time. Catholicism appealed to him as the Corporate power competent to control the exaggerations of individualism. The Catholic Church was a disciplined institution with definite standards of moral life, presenting precisely the qualities of which the individual self so sorely stands in need. The motives of his conversion were neither aesthetic nor sentimental. No ritual attraction drew him to the Church. What made its constraining appeal in his case was the moralizing influence of the religious institution over the waywardness and wilfulness of the natural man.

Religious Thought in France

Brunetière had been under the ascendancy of Taine, revered him as a Master, but ultimately passed beyond the Master's limitations towards the Catholic Religion. His progress was step by step, cautious and slow. The different stages are recorded in a partially autobiographical spirit in the Conferences which he gave during the last decade of the nineteenth century. In a Conference delivered in 1896* he dwelt on the revival of Idealism, a returning consciousness in France that experimental science did not exhaust the sphere of reality, that behind the drama of history and the phenomena of nature there is an Unseen spiritual author—a *Deus absconditus*. Brunetière was convinced of the inadequacy of naturalism or positivism. There were problems in which man was deeply interested and which science was unable to solve. The meaning of life, the purpose for which we exist, the significance of death, were questions which illustrate the futility of the opinion which declared that there were no mysteries remaining. The literary man had come to appreciate keenly the stifling results of restricting reality to the sphere of material science. He saw in the revival of idealism in literature, in music, and in social theories that men were escaping from the limits of materialism towards the sphere of religion.

Three years later he delivered another Conference on the necessity of faith. He criticized shrewdly the popular belief in Progress. Men believed in Progress,

* *Discours de Combat*, tome i.

The Literary Men attracted to the Church

unreservedly, blindly. That only showed that an element of faith entered into the very composition of the human spirit and that in some form or another it was always reappearing. Men could not rid themselves of the necessity of faith. Belief in Progress may be an illusion. It is in any case an uncertainty. But men believe in it. Faith is rooted in the heart of man. Denial does not destroy it. If you don't believe in the Word of God you will believe in the word of man. If you don't believe in the supernatural you will believe in the marvellous. If you don't believe in the spiritual you will believe in the material. Brunetière spoke with the earnestness of conviction that life became superficial if it did not imply eternal relations. But such relations faith alone can secure. There can be no morals without faith, and faith if it is to deserve the name, implies the eternal.

Brunetière was revolted by the levities of Renan. Comte, on the contrary, he acknowledged as, in spite of his errors and extravagances, the great thinker of the past century. Then Brunetière proceeded to claim on Positivist principles the significance of Christian Religion as an objective fact. There is found in Christianity a social and civilizing power which no other religion presents. It has accomplished what no other religion has. It is unique.

Here, however, in a very tantalizing way, Brunetière refrained from conclusions. He claimed that he had availed himself of the grounds which positivism provided for advancing from the subjective to the objective. But he declined on this occasion to enter the sphere of theology. This was as far as he had for the present advanced. And he closed with the hopeful interrogation, why he should not some day or other take another and more decisive step.

Brunetière's whole development was in the direction of the Catholic Faith. If he had lived longer there can be little doubt that he would have arrived. But, as Henri Bremond says, it was a case of obvious tendencies, not of achievement. It was a process whose consummation death prevented.

It must be frankly confessed that among the Conversions to Catholicism in nineteenth-century France are examples which, while they yield unhesitating veneration to the superiority of the moral ideals and resources of the Christian Religion over the prevalent morals and ideals of the world outside, betray a disregard of the tremendous Dogmas on which the morals of that Religion are based, a disregard which is unintelligent and disconcerting.

INDEX

Abelard, theory of Trinity, 148
Acta Apostolicae Sedis, 1921, on Bible, 132–3
Affre, Archbishop of Paris, 155
Atonement, doctrine of (Rivière), 145
Augustine, S., analysis of Love, 147
Augustinian maxim, 130
Authority in Religion, 86

Babbitt, Irving—
  on Bourget, 181
  on Brunetière, 183
Bampton Lectures at S. Paul's, and d'Hulst, 174
Batiffol, Pierre—
  critic of Loisy, 94
  Eucharist and Church, 139
  School of positive Theology, 149
  his *Eucharistie* put on *Index*, 150
  Primitive Catholicism, 151
  sympathy with English Church, 152
  Papal Authority, 152
Baudrillart, on d'Hulst and Loisy, 91, 171
Bellamy, Catholic historian, 129
Bergson—
  influence over sceptical thought in France, 178
  L'Evolution Créatrice, 122
  La Morale et La Religion, 122
Biblical criticism—
  and Faith, 98
  d'Hulst, 172
  Pius IX, 1909, 131

Bossuet, vengeful Deity, 145
Bourget—
  novelist, psychologist, 180
  Le Disciple, 181
Boutroux, Emile, Religion of Humanity, 14, 178
Brémond, Abbé H.—
  friend of Loisy, von Hügel, Tyrrell, 134
  L'Inquiétude Religieuse, 135
  on Newman, development, 135
  funeral of Tyrrell, 136
  Life of S. Chantal, 136
  L'Abbé Tempête (de Rancé), 137
  Sentiment Religieux en France, 138
Brunetière—
  Revue des Deux Mondes, 182
  Essays, *Le Roman Naturaliste*, 182
  History of French Literature, 183
  revival of Idealism, 184
  necessity of Faith, 184
  Belief in Progress, illusion, 184
  Renan's levities, 185
  did not reach full belief, 186

Caro—
  on Comte, 14, 16
  on Littré, 15
Catholicism—
  and Protestantism, 83
  and Infallibility, 85
Chateaubriand, *Génie du Christianisme*, 179

Religious Thought in France

Christianity, value of, to Taine, 19
Church of Humanity at Newcastle, 21
Church obstruction to intellectual development, 90
Comte, Auguste—
  Positivist Religion, 9, 108
  New Religion: two Dogmas, 13
  Definition of Prayer, 22
Congreve, 21
Couchoud—
  The Mystery of Jesus, 62, 150
  agrees with Strauss, Renan, Loisy, 63
  the human Jesus, 83
Cousin, Victor, *History of Philosophy*, 25
Creation, God, Love, 125
Cross, the, on the Pantheon, 166
Cross means Liberty, Civilization, Christianity, 166

Darboy, Archbishop, appoints Père Hyacinthe, 164
D'Hulst, Mgr.—
  and Loisy, 90
  Question biblique, 129
  at Notre Dame, 172
Delvolvé, Rationalism and Tradition, 116
de Quélen, Mgr., Conferences, Paris, 155
de Régnon, on Holy Trinity, 139, 146
de Vaux, Clotilde, Comte's infatuation, 14
Didon, Père, Dominican, 172
Dogma in France, 139

Dogmas, significance of, 85
Dogmatic formulas, disregard of, 149
Dominic, S., Priory of, 23
Doubt and Faith (Guyau), 114
Duchesne—
  and Loisy, 90
  History of the Church, 133
  Les Eglises séparées, 153
Dupanloup, Vicar-General, 155

Eliot, George, ref. Comte, 10
Eucharist, Christ in the (Möhler), 140
L'Evangile et L'Eglise (Loisy), 94

Faith—
  return to, Bourget, Coppée, etc., 178
  Les Grands Convertis (Guignebert), 178
Félix—
  preacher at Notre Dame, 162
  Progress by Christianity, 162
Fichte, personality is a limitation, 26
Fonsegrive, Christian Philosophy, 127
Frommel, Gaston—
  Christianity and Redemption, 75
  sinless perfection of Christ, 75

Gaume, Benedictine edition of Fathers, 133
Giraud, Victor, on Taine, education of children, 20
God, argument for existence of (Saisset), 27

188

Index

Godet, Frederic—
  on S. John, 31, 36
  Conferences on Christian Faith, 37
Gore, Bishop, and Batiffol, 153
Goyau, 139
Grandmaison, Léonce de—
  Deity of Christ, 139
  Christ, Person, Message, 144
Gregory XVI, Pope, and Cousin, 25
Gregory, S., Love between Two, 147
Grétillat, Evangelical Doctrine, 30
Guignebert, Biblical Institute, 132
Guizot—
  on Comte, 12
  spiritualist philosophy, 24
  on A. Monod, 35
  on Lacordaire in Notre Dame, 157, 160
  Ravignon, 161
Guyau—
  Irreligion of the Future, 107
  rejects Catholic Incarnation and Redemption, 109
  Asceticism and obsession of sin, 109
  Christian Religion indispensable, 109
  education of priests in botany, music etc., as against, recital of Breviary, 110
  Home religion and education of child, 110
  Freethinking and Catholic, problem, 111
  restriction of family—celibacy of priests, 112
  on Möhler's *Symbolism*, 139

Harnack—
  Essence of Christianity (Loisy), 94
  on Batiffol's *Primitive Catholicism*, 151
Harrison, Frederic, 21
Hebert, Marcel, gives up Orders, 97
Hefele, *Councils of the Church*, 134
Hibbert Journal, on Loisy, 104
Huxley, Catholicism minus Christianity, 14
Hyacinthe, Père (Loyson)—
  at Notre Dame, 164
  excommunicated, 168
Huysmans, the cathedral, 179

Icard, College of S. Sulpice, 90
Infallibility—
  not Pope alone (Batiffol), 153
  decree, effect on Père Hyacinthe, 165
Inge, Dean of S. Paul's, Loisy's Rationalism, 94
Inspiration of Scripture (Loisy), 92
Irénikon, ref. Pope and Episcopate, 153

James, William, Religious experience, and Bergson, 124
Janvier—
  at Notre Dame 1903, 174
  moral laws of the Church, 175
  consecration of Montmartre Church, 176
  popularity, all classes attracted, 176

Kant, Faith and Reason, 114
Kidd, Dr., review of Batiffol's *Catholicisme et Papanté*, 153

Labertonnière, Christian philosophy, 149
Lacordaire, Abbé, orator, 155-7
Lagrange, Dominican School of Jerusalem, 131-3
Lamennais, Freethinker, 155
Lamentabile, Papal Bull, 96
Lebreton—
  Deity of Christ, 139
  Holy Trinity, 142
  uses Sanday and Swete, 142
Lecky, W. H.—
  European Morals, 120
  on Père Félix, 163
Leo XIII, Question biblique, 129
Lepin, Professor, survey of Couchoud, 64
Le Roy, Edouard, on Bergson, 127
Levy-Bruhl, on Comte, 9
Lewes, George, Comte's influence, 10
Liddon, Dr. H. P.—
  on Félix at Notre Dame, 163
  warning against Hyacinthe's teaching, 165
Littré—
  disciple of Comte, 9
  his religious wife—education of daughter, 16
Loisy—
  S. Paul's view of Jesus, 65
  Autobiography, 89
  Proverbs of Solomon, 90
  his *noms de plume*, 93

Loisy—*continued*
  his attitude to Religion, 96
  excommunicated 1908, 97
  La Naissance du Christianisme, 99
  fiction, legend, myth, 100
  Barabbas, a fiction, 102
Luddy, Ailbe, *The real de Rancé*, 137
Lyttelton, Canon W. H., translated Godet's *Lectures on the Christian Faith*, 37

Malines, Conversations at, 152
Margival, becomes a layman, 97
Married life (Delvolvé), 118
Ménégoz—
  Doctrine of Trinity rejected, 54
  Salvation, what consists in, 69
  death of Christ not sacrificial, 71
  Salvation by Faith, 72
Mercier, Cardinal, 152
Merry del Val, Cardinal, 95-6
Migne, Abbé, Greek and Latin Patrology, 133
Mill, J. S., influenced by Comte 10, 21
Möhler, *Symbolism*, 139
Modernist movement in France, 89
Monod, Adolphe, French Protestant, 34
Monod, Wilfred, "Jesus the layman," 74
Monsabré—
  at Notre Dame (Dogma), 167
  Christ and the poor, 170
  applause at Notre Dame, 171

Index

Montalembert—
  Lacordaire as preacher, 159
  Père Hyacinthe, 164
Morality in Religion, 117–21

Napoleon, on Religion in France, 29
Neuchatel, Protestant School at, 31
Newman, *Essay on Development*, 135

Pascal—
  Provincial Letters, Taine gives to his children, 21
  Protestant unbelief in Eucharist, 107
Pascendi Dominici Gregis 1907, 96
Pattison, Mark, visit to Comtist Service, 114
Petre, Miss, *Life of Tyrrell*, 136
Pius IX, *Syllabus*, 164
Pontius Pilate, crucified under, only article of Creed Loisy believes, 93
Positivism dead in 1883 (Caro says), 16
Positivist philosophy in England, 21
Protestantism—
  in France, remarkable men, 29
  and Scripture, 84–5
Protestant individualism, 86–7
Providentissimus Deus (Leo XIII), 92
Purcell, *Life of Cardinal Manning*, 135

Quin, Malcolm, *Memoir of a Positivist*, 21

Rampolla, Cardinal, 93
Ravignan, at Notre Dame, 160
Religion and Intellect (Bergson), 123
Religious experiences, 124–6
Resurrection, evidences of, 144
Réville, Albert—
  Dogma of Deity of Christ, 47
  exponent of Liberal Protestantism, 50
  rejects doctrine of Trinity, 52
Revival of Religion, if new, or unification of existing ones, 113
Revue du Clergé Français, 93
Richard, S.—
  Nature of Love (Trinity), 147
  Divine Perfection, 147
Richard, Cardinal, and Loisy, 92–4, 171
Rideau, Emile, *Le Dieu de Bergson*, 122
Rivière, Doctrine of Atonement, 145
Roman Catholicism inconsistent with modern science, 20

Sabatier, Auguste—
  newer liberal critical school, 39
  a Huguenot, 41
  religious authority and unity of spirit, 42
  Christians, each prophet, priest, king, 44
  Person of Christ, problem of, 45
  book about S. Paul, 56
  reality of Damascus gate, 57
  Christ potentially Divine; not God, 58

Saisset, Emile—
  Natural Religion, 26
  translated S. Augustine's *City of God*, 27
Sanders, Miss, *Life of S. Chantal*, 136
Scepticism in France (Saisset on), 27
Scherer, Edmund—
  Essay on the Church, 78
  unity of the Church, Invisible, 79
  Anglican belief in Visible Church, 80
  English Church characteristics, 82
  Protestantism in France, 84
Sibour, Archbishop of Paris, 25
Simon, Jules, *Le Devoir*, 25
Sonship of Christ according to S. Paul, 144
Sonship of Christ and of Disciples, 142
S.P.C.K., Brémond's *History of Religion in France*, 138
Spencer, Herbert, ref. Comte, 10, 122
Spiritualist philosophy, five exponents of, 24
Stapfer, Taine's education of children, 20

Suffering Deity, Couchoud says S. Peter's imagination, 100

Taine, Hippolyte—
  belief of, 17
  studied M. Aurelius, Spinoza, Hegel, 18
  influenced by Religion in England, 18
  on Brunetière, 184
Three Heavenly Witnesses (1 S. John v. 7), 130
Tixeront, *History of Dogma*, 134
Trinity, The Holy, Baptismal formula explicit, 143
Troeltch, approves Loisy's Gospel and Church, 94
Turmel, *History of Positive Theology*, 150

Veuillot, Louis, Janvier's panegyric on, 176
Vigoureux, 90, 129
Vinet, Alexandre, 30
von Hügel, Loisy's Gospel and Church, 94-6

Ward, Ideal, 135
Ward, Mrs., *One Poor Scruple*, 135

For Product Safety Concerns and Information please contact our EU representative GPSR@taylorandfrancis.com
Taylor & Francis Verlag GmbH, Kaufingerstraße 24, 80331 München, Germany

www.ingramcontent.com/pod-product-compliance
Lightning Source LLC
Chambersburg PA
CBHW061447300426
44114CB00014B/1878